Sonya Kelly's Druid Plays

Sonya Kelly is an Irish writer and actor. She has performed with all the major Irish companies including the Gate Theatre, Druid Theatre and The Corn Exchange and Fishamble: the new play company. She is a cast member of RTE's hugely successful, sketch show, *The Savage Eye*. Her debut solo show, *The Wheelchair on My Face*: a look back at a myopic childhood, won a Scotsman Fringe First Award for new writing at the Edinburgh Fringe 2012. The show played 150 performances in over fifty venues and toured to Paris and New York where it received a Critic's Pick in the *New York Times*.

Sonya Kelly's Druid Plays

Furniture
Once Upon a Bridge
The Last Return

SONYA KELLY

methuen | drama

LONDON · NEW YORK · OXFORD · NEW DELHI · SYDNEY

METHUEN DRAMA
Bloomsbury Publishing Plc
50 Bedford Square, London, WC1B 3DP, UK
1385 Broadway, New York, NY 10018, USA
29 Earlsfort Terrace, Dublin 2, Ireland

BLOOMSBURY, METHUEN DRAMA and the Methuen Drama logo are
trademarks of Bloomsbury Publishing Plc

First published in Great Britain 2025

Copyright © Sonya Kelly, 2025

Sonya Kelly has asserted her right under the Copyright, Designs and Patents Act,
1988, to be identified as author of this work.

Cover design: Matt Thame

All rights reserved. No part of this publication may be reproduced or transmitted
in any form or by any means, electronic or mechanical, including photocopying,
recording, or any information storage or retrieval system, without
prior permission in writing from the publishers.

Bloomsbury Publishing Plc does not have any control over, or responsibility for,
any third-party websites referred to or in this book. All internet addresses given in this book
were correct at the time of going to press. The author and publisher regret any inconvenience
caused if addresses have changed or sites have ceased to exist, but can accept no
responsibility for any such changes.

No rights in incidental music or songs contained in the work are hereby granted
and performance rights for any performance/presentation whatsoever
must be obtained from the respective copyright owners.

All rights whatsoever in this play are strictly reserved and application
for performance etc. should be made before rehearsals to Curtis Brown Group Ltd.,
Haymarket House, 28-29 Haymarket, London, SW1Y 4SP. No performance may
be given unless a licence has been obtained.

A catalogue record for this book is available from the British Library.

A catalog record for this book is available from the Library of Congress.

ISBN: HB: 978-1-3505-0035-8
PB: 978-1-3505-0034-1
ePDF: 978-1-3505-0037-2
eBook: 978-1-3505-0036-5

Series: Methuen Drama Play Collections

Typeset by Newgen KnowledgeWorks Pvt. Ltd., Chennai, India
Printed and bound in Great Britain

To find out more about our authors and books visit www.bloomsbury.com
and sign up for our newsletters.

Contents

Introduction by Garry Hynes   vii

Furniture   1

Once Upon a Bridge   57

The Last Return   121

Introduction

Sonya's history with Druid stretches back over twenty years and began not as a writer but as an actor. In 1998 she made her Druid acting debut as Nóra in *The Way You Look Tonight* by Niall Williams and then returned in 2004 to play one of the village girls in *The Playboy of the Western World* by J. M. Synge, sharing the stage with Anne-Marie Duff, Cillian Murphy and Chris O'Dowd.

With her early plays for Fishamble Theatre Company, she burst forth onto the Irish and international stage as a playwright with a universal yet entirely unique perspective and, in doing so, won the hearts of audiences and the praise of critics the world over.

Sonya's return to Druid happened via our New Writing programme. In 2016 she submitted the script for her third play, *Furniture*, to our open script submission window where it was read anonymously and selected to be one of two scripts from hundreds of submissions to be performed as part of our annual Druid Debuts rehearsed reading series the following summer at Galway International Arts Festival.

After the success of that rehearsed reading, we put the play into full production and it received its world premiere in the summer of 2018 at The Mick Lally Theatre, Druid's home in Galway. A national tour soon followed in the spring of 2019.

In the summer of 2020, while the world was in lockdown, we commissioned Sonya to write a new play for us which became *Once Upon a Bridge*. A play of unexpected collisions and connections, Sonya's writing united audiences all over the world when we live streamed the production from Galway to homes in thirty-four countries in February 2021.

The next year we premiered *The Last Return*, her most ambitious play yet, which opened in Galway in July 2022, quickly transferred to Traverse Theatre for Edinburgh Festival Fringe, then spent a month at Dublin's Gate Theatre and, the following spring, toured all over Ireland. Along the way, Sonya picked up a Scotsman Fringe First Award and was a finalist for the prestigious Susan Smith Blackburn Prize.

I don't know any other writer like Sonya Kelly and I don't think I ever will. She is a singular talent, who brings humour and humanity to the stage and screen, powered by a vivid imagination and a passionate determination. I'm so proud that Druid has played a part in her rise to success and I look forward to our partnership continuing for years to come.

Garry Hynes
May 2024

Druid

Founded in 1975, Druid is a touring theatre company, anchored in the West of Ireland and looking to the world. Druid passionately believes that audiences have the right to see first-class professional theatre in their own communities. The company has toured the length and breadth of Ireland, as well as touring internationally to the UK, United States, Canada, Australia, New Zealand, Japan and Hong Kong.

Since 1975, Druid's work has both celebrated the theatrical canon and championed new writers. Production highlights from the company's 49-year history include its play cycles such as DruidSynge, DruidMurphy, DruidShakespeare and DruidO'Casey, and The Beauty Queen of Leenane which, during its run on Broadway, won four Tony Awards, including Best Director for Garry Hynes, the first woman to win an award for directing in the history of the Tony Awards.

The company has nurtured some of the most significant names in Irish writing, and continues to commission and develop future generations of theatre makers through its new writing and artist development programmes. At the heart of its artistic programme is the Druid Ensemble who work closely with Artistic Director Garry Hynes and the Druid team to deliver a bold programme of Irish and international work.

'one of the world's great acting ensembles' – *The Guardian*

'a world-class company rooted in the cultural fabric of Galway'
 – *The Irish Times*

'Ireland's most prestigious theatre company' – *Irish Independent*

'the most successful Irish theatrical export ever' – *Irish Independent*

'any New York visit by the Druid Theatre Company of Galway is an
 event not to be missed' – *The New York Times*

Druid gratefully acknowledges the support of the Arts Council of Ireland, Smurfit Kappa and the University of Galway, and many other funders, supporters and donors.

Druid
Flood Street, Galway, Ireland
www.druid.ie
@druidtheatre

Furniture

Furniture was first presented by Druid in 2017 as a Druid Debut rehearsed reading, the company's annual series of rehearsed readings of new plays. In 2018, it received its world premiere production at The Mick Lally Theatre, Druid's home in Galway, followed by a national tour of Ireland in 2019.

'wickedly insightful' – *The Irish Times*
'laugh-out-loud funny' – *The Sunday Times*
'whip smart ... a triumph' – *Irish Independent*

Druid Debuts rehearsed reading, 2017:

Cast

George	**Niall Buggy**
Ed	**Shane O'Reilly**
Michael	**Paul Curley**
Alex	**Janet Moran**
Dee	**Rebecca O'Mara**
Stef	**Aisling O'Sullivan**

World premiere at The Mick Lally Theatre, 2018:

Cast

George	**Niall Buggy**
Ed	**Peter Campion**
Michael	**Garrett Lombard**
Alex	**Clare Monnelly**
Dee	**Rebecca O'Mara**
Stef	**Aisling O'Sullivan**

Creative Team

Writer	Sonya Kelly
Director	Cathal Cleary
Designer	Francis O'Connor
Lighting Designer	Sinéad McKenna
Sound Designer	Greg Clarke

Irish tour, 2019:

Cast

George	**Niall Buggy**
Ed	**Rory Nolan**
Michael	**Garrett Lombard**
Alex	**Kate Kennedy**
Dee	**Ruth McGill**
Stef	**Helen Norton**

Furniture

A play by

Sonya Kelly
for Druid Theatre 2019

Characters

Play One: Bibendum

Ed, *a man in his thirties or forties.*
Alex, *in her thirties*

Play Two: La-Z-Boy

Stef, *a woman*
Dee, *a woman*

Play Three: Chaise Longue

George, *a man over seventy*
Michael, *a man in his thirties or forties*

Notes

A dash indicates a short pause, a new thought, or a change in energy.

Bona Polari glossary

Palone-omi – Butch dyke
Feeles – Children
Naff – Ugly
Eek – Face
Lallies – Legs

Play One

Bibendum

An exhibition space. Among the items is an Eileen Grey Bibendum armchair and an E1027 chrome side table.

We hear distant the low burble of a small social gathering.

Alex *and* **Ed** *enter. They have brochures. Along with her handbag,* **Alex** *carries a small gift bag. They take in their surroundings.*

We hear a tap on a microphone and the banter hushes. We hear an off-stage **Voice***.* **Alex** *and* **Ed** *face outwards to listen.*

Voice *(O/S)*   Ladies and gentlemen, please welcome the Minister for the Arts.

Soft applause. **Alex** *claps.* **Ed** *doesn't.*

Minister *(O/S)*   Thank you. You are all very welcome to the opening of ... Legacy, a unique exhibition celebrating some of the world's most innovative pieces of interior design. And such remarkable roll call of artists, including, the master of the bentwood chair Thonet ... Thonet? Is it?

Ed   Toe-net ...

Minister *(O/S)*   Thonet ... Michael Thonet –

Ed   *Mich-elle.*

Alex   Shush.

Ed   She said it wrong.

Alex   So?

Minister *(O/S)*   Miss Michelle Thonet ... And also Gio Panti ...

Voice *(O/S)*   Ponti.

Minister *(O/S)*   Gio Ponti, and the serene elegance of Miss Eileen Grey. Artists whose work has transcended their humble utilitarian purpose to become timeless works of art in their own right. And I have to say, does it not make you want to dash home and redo the living room. Ha, ha ...

Ed *shakes his head in despair.* **Alex** *looks at him.*

6   Furniture

Minister (*O/S*)   So, I officially declare this exhibition open.

Soft applause.

Please enjoy your afternoon with these very beautiful things, in light of which, may I propose a toast: to beautiful things.

Alex   To beautiful things.

Soft applause.

Alex   Hooray!

Ed (*wtf*)   Hooray?

Alex   What?

Ed   Hooray.

Alex   Yes, to beautiful things, hooray.

Ed   Hooray? (*Looking round him.*) Alex come on.

Alex   Okay, relax.

Ed   Yeah, I know, jus … hooray?

Alex (*shuts it down*)   Happy anniversary.

Ed   Yes.

–

Happy anniversary.

–

Hooray.

Seeing **Alex**'s *bag.*

Is that a present?

Alex   Yes.

Ed   For me?

Alex   Uh-huh.

Ed   A present for me.

Alex   Yes.

Ed   You got me a present for *me*?

Play One: Bibendum   7

Alex Yes, I did. I got *you* a present for you. Don't look so scared.

Ed But I didn't get you a present. Balls.

Alex Don't say balls when someone gets you a present.

–

It doesn't matter you didn't get a present for me.

Ed We don't normally do presents, do we?

Alex No, *we* don't.

Ed I mean, if I'd known, if you'd said, I'd have got you a present but …
we didn't to the thing where we said what the plans were going to be.

Alex And?

Ed And now I look like a dick.

Alex Ed. Dick. Please. It's not a competition. This isn't an us thing, it's
just a *me* thing so don't go all … you-y on me.

Ed I wasn't.

–

And you look nice, by the way, I didn't say it earlier not because I didn't
notice … I just didn't want a compliment about your looks to be the first
thing I said.

Alex Well, that's very thoughtful of you.

Ed Thanks.

Alex Feminism thanks you.

Ed –

Alex Betty Friedan just came in her grave.

Ed Alex, I'm being nice, don't take the piss.

Alex Sorry.

Ed 'S fine.

–

Well, can I have it?

Alex Have what?

8   Furniture

Ed   The thing, the present.

Alex   No.

Looks over at other guests.

I want to give it to you when we're alone.

Ed   Ah, come on. You can't just buy me a present and not give it to me because I didn't buy you one.

Alex   That is not why I am not giving it to you. Listen when I speak. I said I would give it to you later.

Ed *tries to swipe the gift out of* **Alex***'s hand but she pulls it away.*

Alex (*putting gift into handbag*)   No I said!

Ed   Ah …

Alex   I am not competing with a load of old chairs and tables. Go on. (*Nods to crowd.*) Go and network.

Ed   Eh, no.

Alex   Go and mingle.

Ed   I don't want to mingle.

Alex   What's the point in coming here if you're not going to mingle –

Ed   Eh, you tell me.

Alex   – If we're just going to hide in the corner like a pair of –

Ed   Pair of what?

Alex   –

Ed   *I* didn't want to come here. *You* wanted to come here.

Alex   I wanted to come here to do something nice for *you*.

Ed   And *I* accepted to do something nice for *you* … because it's our anniversary.

–

I didn't even know we were invited.

Alex   We weren't.

Ed (*panics, looks around him*)   What?!

Play One: Bibendum 9

Alex We're gate-crashing!

Ed Jesus, Alex!

Alex Oh, come on, Ed!

Ed Come on, we're going.

Alex But you used to love doing this –

Ed (*pulling her*) Now, out –

Alex (*pulling back*) Stealing the little sculpture food, bottle of wine in the handbag –

Ed Out, now –

Alex No.

Ed Come on.

Alex I'm not going.

–

You *love* this. Go schmooze and mingle. Go schmingle! (*Points to* **Minister**.) Get your picture taken with the Minister.

Ed (*pushes her hand down*) Eh, no thank you!

Alex Be good for your profile.

Ed Alex, please.

Alex What about him with the tortoiseshell glasses. Go talk to him.

Ed No way. I am *not* talking to him.

Alex Didn't you meet him about putting your stuff in his gallery?

Ed Putting my stu . . . Putting my *stuff* in his gallery?

Alex Okay, wrong term.

Ed Eh, in the art world it's called, showing your work?

Alex Well, didn't you meet him about *showing your work?*

Ed Eh … yes but …

Alex Well then you should go say hi.

Ed I can't, it's … it's … tricky.

Alex Why is it tricky? Just go say hi.

10   Furniture

Ed   No. look, you're not an artist, you wouldn't get it but … if he hasn't come to a decision yet, it could be tricky.

—

If *he's* already said yes in his head and not told me, then it's … tricky for *him* because he doesn't know if *I'm* thinking yes or no and not told *him*. On the other hand if *I've* said no in my head but not told *him* then it's tricky for me. So you see it's …

Alex   Tricky.

Ed   Yes.

Alex   Is tricky code for, you've said no?

Ed   No! I haven't said *no*, well I haven't *not* said no. I don't know.

Alex   And sorry, why is it tricky for him?

Ed   'Cause there's boards and stuff … People you have to go through, you wouldn't get it. Besides, I'm not sure my work is right for his walls.

Alex   Not right for his walls.

Ed   Yeah it could be all wrong.

Alex   Fine. And I *do* get it by the way. *And* I do know what a board is. I am answerable to one.

Ed   On what?

Alex   On what flavour biscuits to have in the canteen!

Ed   Shush!

Alex   On my job!

Ed   Okay.

Alex   What do you think?

Ed   Fine.

Alex   It's *very* tricky.

Ed   Look, I'm sorry. Just, you know. We're here now. Let's just enjoy ourselves and not try to fix the world.

Alex   Sure. It's our anniversary. Here's to beautiful things and not fixing the world.

Play One: Bibendum   11

Ed   Cheers.

Pause.

Ed   Pieces, by the way.

Alex   Huh?

Ed   You say pieces, not things.

Alex   Did I just say things?

Ed   Yes.

Alex   Oh.

–

She said things.

Ed   Did she?

Alex   The Minister, yes, she said, 'Here's to beautiful things.' And then we said it after her. She *said* it twice, actually.

Ed   She *read* it twice, actually.

Alex   Yeah, well, how was she to know?

Ed   It's her job to know.

Alex   –

She looks around her, sees the Bibendum chair and walks toward it.

Oh look, now that *is* beautiful.

Ed   Don't touch it.

Alex   I'm sorry?

Ed   No … it's just … you know, don't touch it.

Alex   I wasn't going to touch it.

Ed   That's an original 1926 original Bibendum chair by Eileen Gray.

Alex   I know. I can read. And?

Ed   And you were moving towards it.

Alex   Yeah, *and* –

Ed   *And* so you were going to touch it.

12   Furniture

Alex   No I wasn't.

Ed   You had your hand out.

Alex   I said, 'Wow, that's beautiful.' Then I leaned in to get a better look.

Ed   You had your hand out like you were going to touch it.

Alex   I had my hand out *like* I was going to touch it. That doesn't mean I was going to touch it. Besides, you weren't even looking at me. You were looking over at Mr Tortoiseshell with the … wrong walls.

Ed   Well, all I'm saying is why would you put your hand out as if you were going to touch something if you weren't going to touch it?

Alex   It's a superfluous gesture, you know, 'Wow. There's a cool chair near that coffee table …'

Ed   Side table.

Alex   Side table, whatever.

Ed   Coffee tables are lower –

Alex   And you know, like ta-da! There it is. Hand gesture. Big deal. It doesn't mean I'm going to touch it.

Ed   Well, it didn't look that way to me. I'm just saying don't touch it.

Alex   And I'm just saying, get over yourself. Why am I even explaining myself to you? I'm a grown woman. I'm not a child in a china shop.

Ed   Fine.

Alex   Fine?

Ed   Yeah, fine. You weren't going to touch it then.

Alex   Fine? What is *with* you?

Ed (*shush hand gesture*)

Alex   You just asked – no – ordered a grown woman, not to touch an art exhibit. Fine? Eh, 'Darling, I am so sorry. I don't know what I was thinking. Of course, you weren't going to touch it. That was just me being really mean there for no reason. I get self-conscious at these things, I'm an artist, I get insecure, I can't help it.'

Ed   Eh, I do so fucking not get insecure at these things.

Alex   Eh, you do so fucking do.

Play One: Bibendum 13

Ed   Like when? Name me one time.

Alex   Apart from now?

Ed   Name me one time – and not apart from now because it isn't one –
that I got insecure at one of these things and *don't* say the –

Ed/Alex   Florian Kee exhibition in the –

Alex   Bois de Boulogne in Paris. I *do* say, actually. Christ, you got your
jocks in a knot.

Ed   Don't st –

Alex   So there we were in a giant exhibition room the size of what,
three tennis courts?

Ed   You beeped.

Alex   All the art world's top people, isn't that right, isn't that what
you said?

Ed   You beeped.

Alex   All wandering round in their Buddy Holly glasses, and their
vintage Chanel fascinators and some classical realism –

Ed   Classical realist.

Alex   Classical realist uber nerd gets a little too near a table made out
of dead foxes and beep! It's all my fault.

Ed   I turned, and you were over the line when the thing went off. You
beeped. There's no beep machine here, that's why I *had* to say don't
touch it just now, because I clearly remember in the Bois de Boulogne
you beeped.

Alex   I did not beep. You *assumed* I beeped. Out of the hundred or so
people who could have also beeped, *you* assumed *I*, the art pleb beeped.

Ed   Your foot was over the line.

Alex   My foot was not over the line.

Ed   Your foot was over the line.

Alex   You were three tennis courts away, you couldn't possibly see if my
foot was over the line.

Ed   Your foot was *touching* the line.

Alex   No it fucking wasn't because you know why?

14   Furniture

Ed   Keep. Your voice. Down.

Alex   'Cause you know why? I'm not that pushed on getting up close and personal with tables made out of dead foxes. That's why. It's gross. You weren't even looking at me. You were too busy star fucking Mr. Florian Klee –

Ed   Florian Kee –

Alex   Had your head so far up his ass he was smiling with two sets of teeth.

–

And because do you know why else? If it *had* been me, I'd have beeped and I'd have said, 'Oops, sorry. That was me. No one died. Except for the foxes.' But I didn't beep so I didn't say anything because it wasn't *me*.

Ed   Was.

Alex   Wasn't.

Ed   Was.

Alex   Wasn't!

Ed   Was!

Alex   It wasn't. What are you, ten?

Ed   Eh, *no* because that would make *you* a paedophile.

–

And for your information, that piece of art was called *Fox Table*, not *a table made out of foxes*. A table made out of foxes is just a table made out of foxes. Fox *Table* is a priceless work of art by Florian *Kee*.

Alex   Well, soh-ree.

Ed   I would just appreciate it if you made more of an effort to respect my professional vernacular, that's all.

Alex   Right.

Ed   Fox Table is not a table for use in the traditional sense of the word. The artist was taking a stereotypical inanimate icon of contemporary domestic living, and juxtaposing it with an equally iconic animate rural predator in order to examine how the inanimate and seemingly innocuous convenience objects we create in the human world are actually more powerful predators than any living thing, in this case, a fox and a table.

Alex So *Fox Table is* a table.

Ed Ye … ne …

—

The artist took all these intangible ideas see, and, and, and melded them into a physical object designed to unsettle the viewers' perspective of a table and help them come to a more enlightened understanding. The museum at the Bois de Boulogne, being the conduit for this transaction between the object and thousands of viewers, are responsible for its protection, which is why if you go to near it you beep.

Alex So *Fox Table* is *not* a table.

Ed Florian Kee's *Fox Table is* a table but not a *table* table, no.

Alex And Eileen Grey's chair, is that a chair?

Ed Yes. It is a chair.

Alex For sitting on.

Ed Originally, yes.

Alex And now?

Ed And now it has become, important. In the history of innovative furniture design, it is iconic. And in order to preserve its importance as an icon, it became no longer a chair for sitting *on*, but a chair for looking *at*. Its rarity, its originality, its monetary value creates a sense of reverence around the artist that we honour by not touching the work.

Alex Because it's worth a load of money.

Ed N … *because* there's oily secretions, right? Grease in our hands yeah, and, and, and it comes out your fingers and corrodes the objects they touch.

If every person who admired that chair touched that chair, that chair would not exist for future generations to admire in turn as you have. By not touching the chair you are respecting the chair and therefore helping it to survive time itself. People who touch art have no concept of time beyond their own experience of it. They are so stupefied by the myth of the *individual* pumped into them by bastardized Freudian shit box advertising, they think any unfulfilled need is an affront on their basic

16   Furniture

human rights so they go, 'Don't you oppress me by telling me I can't touch something I want to touch, wah, wah, wah. I'm going to assert my human rights.' So they touch it, and thousands upon thousands of *individuals* do the same over centuries until it's touched into non-existence.

And then they go, 'Oh, where did the lovely chair go? Oh, never mind. Look there's the Mona Lisa. I wonder what it's like to lick her face?'

Alex   And you hate those people.

Ed   Yes.

Alex   People who touch things they're not supposed to touch.

Ed   I'm an artist. Of course I hate those people.

Alex   And you're worried –

Ed   Am I worried? They are ignorant, selfish, greasy philistines eroding cultural legacy with their very fingertips. Of course I'm worried.

Alex   You're worried that one of those people is me.

Ed   –

No!

Alex   Then why would you say, 'Don't touch it,' if you were certain that I wouldn't?

Ed   It's just something you say!

Alex   You are worried you married someone who doesn't know how to behave around priceless furniture. That's why you said, 'Don't touch it.' You weren't just scared of me touching it. You were scared of me being the type of person who would.

Ed   Of course no! It's just in the Bois de Boulogne you beeped and –

Alex   And you don't want to feel like that today, because it's our anniversary. You don't want to feel the way you did in the Bois de Boulogne when you went down on one knee by the lake, and I said yes. And I was so happy 'cause we'd just come out of that really shitty phase when I'd just qualified, and you got that review. And we both weren't sure, but never really said because we secretly thought whatever it was would pass. I thought we were going to disappear into the bushes and make love but then you took me to that exhibition and I indulged you because I was so happy even though secretly I thought it was a bit selfish. And then the fucking thing went beep and you thought, 'Oh god, what

Play One: Bibendum   17

have I done? I have entangled myself with a woman who beeps. What if I get famous? What if I become the toast of Europe like the fantastic Mr. Foxtable? She'll touch and beep and say *hooray* and *things* instead of *pieces* and she'll mortify me.'

—

And while we are on the subject of *mort*ality, just so you know, because I've a first-class honours degree in medicine so I do, everything is finite Ed. You, me and everyone we know. Even the very concept of art is finite because it was created by humans and they're finite. That is a beautiful chair. One day it will no longer exist and you can wrap that up in as much art speak as you like and tie it up in a big fucking bow, it's never going to change that. We are carbon on a conveyor belt. That is all.

Ed   And that stops us from wanting to protect beautiful pieces?

Alex   Right.

—

How important, how important is protecting that chair from finger grease in comparison to all the other living things in life that are worth protecting?

Ed   Oh, here we go —

Alex   Like me.

Ed   Oh no —

Alex   *If* I suddenly felt unwell and needed to sit down, would you tell me not to sit in the chair?

Ed   Oh, com … I would just get you another chair.

Alex   *If* I suddenly felt unwell and I needed to sit down and there were absolutely no other chairs, for several miles, would you tell me not to sit in the chair?

Ed   That is an utterly toxic hypothetical.

Alex   It is an utterly valid and viable hypothetical.

Ed   Valid to whom?

Alex   Valid to me. I need to know. Which is more important to you, the protection of an artwork for a future generation you will never know, or the protection of a living person you do?

18   Furniture

Ed   Have you gone absolutely mental?

Alex   No, I am asking you a question you find challenging so you are counter questioning my mental health as a defence mechanism.

Ed   Don't you fucking ... wo ... woman-splain to me how my own mind works you ... You know what this is about? Allow me to counter man-splain it to you so we are back on a level playing field. I am passionate about art and you find that threatening. I use words you can't pronounce or explain.

Alex   Yeah?

Ed   Yeah.

Alex   Oh yeah?

Ed   Yeah!

Alex   What do I do for a living?

Ed   –

Oh, very good. Well played. Game and set.

Alex   Come on. What do I do?

Ed   —

You're an eye doctor.

Alex   Sorry?

Ed   You're an eye doctor.

Alex   I am an eye doctor. Very good. And what's the technical term for eye doctor?

Ed   –

You're an opth ...

Alex   Yes?

Ed   You're an optham ...

Alex   Sorry, an ophthal ... what?

Ed   You're an opthalmonologist.

Alex (*laughing*)   Oh really, I'm an opthalmonologist, am I? Well, I simply must let the nee-naw people down the *hostable* know.

Play One: Bibendum   19

Ed   You are a dick.

Alex   Are you actually capable of having a conversation without flinging sex organs in my face?

—

All I am saying is I would just appreciate it if you made more of an effort to respect my *professional vernacular*, that's all. Considering that word you can't be bothered pronouncing properly is what pays our bills.

Ed   You don't have a clue, do you?

Alex   You don't have a *bank account*, do you? Do you?

—

You're on my medical insurance by the way, did you know that? Life assurance too.

Ed   In case of what?

Alex   In case you die. In case you're sick I have to look after …

Ed   Look after whom? Look after whom Alex? After I die, look after whom?

Alex   —

You want to just swan through life without touching the sides, don't you? You just want to wriggle on through like a little worm from magic toilet paper land where miracle milk lands in the fridge and apparitional underpants appear in your drawers and dinners rain from the sky right into your mouth. Any idea how hard I work to pay for it all?

Ed   You have no respect for what I do.

Alex   You have no respect for the fact that the eleven years it took me to learn what I do, fixes the very things that allow people to see what it is you do. You see those two pretty little globes of collagen fibres, and optic nerves and vitreous jelly and photosensitive cells stuck into the front of your face there.

Ed's *focus drifts over to the other guests.* **Alex** *snaps her fingers in front of his face and pulls him back like a schoolboy.*

Alex   Eyes! They're called eyes! And I can fix those eyes with micro tools, repair and stitch them back together with monofilament less than the width of a human hair. I can detect myopia in a six-month-old baby

20   Furniture

who doesn't even have the language facility to say, 'Mummy and Daddy, where are you?'

(*Scoffing at him.*) *You have no respect for what I do.*

—

I restore people's sight with my bare hands! That's what I do! And the money I earn from doing it pays for you to do the thing that you do.

Ed   And that upsets you?

Alex   Of course it upsets me.

Ed   Good. Phew! You've got my back at last, I'm delighted. Why don't you write a letter to the Minister. Oh no wait! Look! She's over there. See! The one you were clapping like a seal shouting hooray at a minute ago. Go on. Go up and tell her she's exploiting your husband. Go up and ask her why she's so happy to get her picture taken with me one day and stick the knife in me the next. Go on love, up you pop. Tell her how you have to subsidize my career with your income because *she* won't anymore!

—

Medical things? You want to talk about medical things, huh?

Alex   Yeah.

Ed   Do you?

Alex   Yeah.

Ed   Do you really?

Alex   Why not?

Ed   Okay. 'Cause you're going to get it now.

—

Why are we here, Alex?

Alex   What's that got to do with medical things?

Ed   Answer the question.

Alex   To have a nice time.

Ed   Wave to the Minister? Say hi to Mr Tortoiseshell?

Alex   I didn't know they'd be –

Ed   Of course you did.

Play One: Bibendum   21

Alex   He said no, didn't he? Mr Tortoiseshell. He said no.

Ed   Of course he said no! You *know* he said no. I *know* he said no. Everyone in this room *knows* he said no! And *that's* why we're here!

—

Because for you to have everything you want, you *need* me to fail. My *lack* of success is part of your plan. 'Cause you're going tickity tick tick, it's time, I can see it in your eyes. You want the nice home with the driveway, and the buzzer gates and the ivy up the side. You want the special basket in the hall for the Wellington boots, and another for the toys.

You want the hobby artist husband who spends his days watching the children from the garden shed while he makes sculptures out of owl feathers, and you're off out there with your micro tools for sixty hours a week, fixing the world. But that's not what I want to be.

Looks at chair.

I want to be *HER*. I want to be great. I want to create beautiful things that exist long after I'm not here.

Alex   Everyone said don't do it, you know. When we came back from Paris, everyone said don't do it. Not in a bad way. Just more … you're doing so well, you've got it all on track, and he's lovely but he'll chew your slippers. Enjoy the fruit. Just … don't climb the tree.

—

Our trouble is not that we're different. Our trouble is we're not different enough.

Opens handbag.

Because I'm going to be *Her*. I'm going to be great at what I do.

Takes out gift.

I'm going to create beautiful things that exist long after I'm not here.

Nodding to chair.

But to truly create, one must first question everything.

*Hooking gift on **Ed**'s fingers.*

Happy anniversary.

Alex *exits.*

22   Furniture

Ed *looks at the bag and opens it. He picks out a ribbon, on the end of which reveals a baby's soother. He lets the bag fall to the floor. He collapses down into the Bibendum chair in shock.*

We hear Orla Fallon sing 'Down by the Sally Gardens'. The scene changes as he exits.

Play Two

La-Z-Boy

A spacious, tastefully decorated open-plan apartment full of fabulous furniture.

There is also a door to a built-in closet. The kitchen is USR. A door that leads to the bedroom is USL.

Stef enters from the kitchen, and moves the chair and table from the previous scene into its new position. She takes a remote out of her pocket and changes the music.

Stef Shut it, Sally, you're wrecking the mood.

On comes 'Love Like This' by Faith Evans. She puts the living room table in place and polishes it to the music.

Stef Uh-huh …

The doorbell rings. She checks her look, dips the music and opens the door to **Dee**. **Dee** *is well dressed in an expensive looking coat. They stand in the doorway staring intensely at each other, like film noir intense.*

Dee Stef.

Stef Dee.

Dee Hi.

Stef Hi.

Dee Someone was leaving so I didn't buzz.

Stef 'S fine.

Dee It's me.

Stef I know.

Dee This is mad.

Stef This *is* mad.

Dee Yeah but fuck it.

Stef Yeah fuck it you know when you know.

Dee Totally. And I so totally know.

Stef Me too. I so totally so know. I know I want to peel you like an orange. I want to neck you like an oyster. I want to slam you like tequila. I want to f … lambé you like a … *crepe suzette.*

24   Furniture

Dee   Stef, the neighbours.

Stef   Fuck 'em they're all queer.

Dee   Yeah?

Stef   You're in the hip district now Dee, even the straight ones are queer.

Dee   Yeah?

Stef   Yeah. You have to pass a special test to get in the building.

Dee   What are the questions?

Stef   What year was Versace shot?

Dee   1997.

Stef   What was Doris Day's real name?

With one hand, **Stef** *undoes a button on* **Dee***'s coat.*

Dee   Mary Anne Kappelhoff.

She undoes another.

Stef   Name those two hot girls from Pussy Riot.

Dee   Nadeshda Tolokonnikova and Maria Alyokhina.

She undoes the belt.

Stef   That's true.

Dee   Yeah, and they're not girls they're women.

Stef   Say their names again.

Dee   Nadeshda Tolokonnikova and Maria Alyokhina.

Stef   Get in here.

Dee   Yeah?

Stef   Get the fuck in here. I am going to bang your total brains out right now this very minute.

Stef *pulls* **Dee** *inside and kicks the door shut without taking her eyes off her.*

Stef   Shoes. Shoes. Shoes.

Dee   Sorry. Sorry. Sorry.

Stef   'S fine.

Play Two: La-Z-Boy   25

Dee (*removing shoes*)   I love you. I so totally fucking love you.

Stef *yanks off* **Dee**'s *coat and tosses it to the floor.*

Stef   I know … I mean I totally so fucking love you too.

Dee (*getting up on table*)   I'm so happy we live in an age where we can make people come out of telephones.

Stef   Me too.

Dee   Like there's nothing you can't order from your phone nowadays. People. Pizza. Sperm.

Right to your front door. It's amazing.

Stef   Yeah, 's amazing. And you are one hot piece of … app.

She goes for **Dee**'s *dress belt.*

Stef   Wait. What are those studs?

Dee   Yeah.

Stef   Off. Off. Off! Get off!

She yanks **Dee** *off the table by the belt.*

Stef   It's eh … mid-century Danish. Stay there. Don't move.

She grabs a rug off the sofa, throws it over the table and flings **Dee** *back on top like a rag doll.*

Stef   Move!

Stef   Get ready, I'm coming in.

Dee   Wait, wait, Stef, Stef, Stef, wait.

Stef   What?

Dee   All my stuff is in the hall. Shouldn't I get it in case, you know, someone thinks it's rubbish.

Stef   They're hardly going to think it's rubbish.

Dee   Come on, I better get it. Please? Then you can bang my total brains out right now this very minute in a minute.

Stef   Yeah?

Dee   Yeah.

Stef   Yeah.

26   Furniture

They get up off the table.

Stef   Okay. Go on, get your stuff! Bring it in! Move it all in! Me casa, tu casa! Ole!

Speaking of which …

Stef *takes a set of keys out of her pocket and hands them to* **Dee**. **Dee** *misses and they land on the table with a clatter.* **Dee** *picks them up.*

Dee   Oops. Sorry.

Stef   Don't worry 's fine.

Dee   Wow. Keys. It's … we're not … it's just, I can't believe we're doing this. I mean it's such a big decision with our lives, I mean …

Stef   Big decision with our lives? It's not a big decision with our lives. I work in human resources, I make big decisions with people's lives every day. Any idea how many times a week I have to say … *I'm so sorry Mr. Blah, we're going to have to let you go.* Nah, not for me it's not a big decision.

Leans in to kiss.

You. Me. Us. Here. No brainer.

Dee (*centimetre from kiss*)   Wow.

Stef   What?

Dee   Human resources.

Kiss is over.

Stef   What about it?

Dee   I … it's just … I thought it … I dunno. *Human, resources.* They're such positive optimistic words on their own. Put then together and …

She examines the keys.

It's not too soon is it?

Stef   A month? Nah! Not when you know.

Dee   And you know when you know.

She looks at the keys again.

Stef   Sure do.

—

Okay, go! Get your stuff 'cause you look so hot right now, I'm going to explode and I've just had the walls redone.

Dee Stuff, yeah. I'll get my stuff.

Stef Just dump it in the closet for tonight.

Dee Okay.

Dee *goes out into the hall.* **Stef** *runs a hand over the table where the keys landed then goes to the kitchen and fixes drinks with her back to the room.*

As the dialogue continues, **Dee** *hauls in her stuff: junk, stacks of it: Grotty old teddy bears, rucksacks, overstuffed Lidl and Aldi bags with broken handles, a giant Jodie Foster poster, all disappear into the closet.* **Stef** *is in the kitchen, oblivious.*

Stef Oh, my god, I forgot to ask. How'd the job interview go?

Dee Ugh, I dunno. Much too corporate for me. Couldn't drink the Kool Aid. You were right about my old job though, it's way too far from here.

Stef *Old* job?

Dee Yeah, I quit.

Stef You quit?

Dee Yep. Besides I'd have to drive, which means I'd have to *learn* and … oh, I dunno, left and right, the stress of all that.

—

Keys. Wow! You know, I've never had a set of keys before, well I did but I never used them.

Stef Did your place not get burgled?

Dee Oh, all the time.

Stef –

You want a drink?

Dee Yes. Whatever you're having.

Stef Well, I *have* everything so you can have what you like.

Dee Nah, I'll just have whatever you're having.

Stef Well, I'm going to make an Old Fashioned for myself. You want one of those?

28   Furniture

Dee   If it's what you're having.

Stef   Okay, last chance to be an individual ...

Dee   There's no such thing.

Stef (*didn't hear*)   You much stuff?

Dee   Yeah ... nah, I dunno. Define much.

She gets the last of the bags, stuffs them in the closet, forces the door shut and goes out again.

Hey, what's in an Old Fashioned anyway?

Stef   Oh, eh, let's see there's three to four dashes of gum syrup, depending on the size of your glass.

Dee *enters pushing a hideous, giant, stained and tattered purple La-Z-Boy chair and places it upstage.*

Stef   Two dashes of Bogart's bitters, one large measure of whiskey, one or two dashes of Curaçao, one small piece of lemon peel, preferably smoked and synged, and a big old-fashioned fistful of ...

She turns.

... holy fuck what's that!

Dee   What's what?

Stef   What's that? What's that there?

Dee   Oh that, sorry, that's my chair.

Stef   Oh ... okay ... ha ...

Dee   Wait, one more thing.

She takes the magazine rack from beside the sofa and places it beside the chair.

Ta-dah! That's me! I am officially moved in! Lock stock and barrel.

No going back now.

Stef   No going back now. No ... going ... back ...

—

Did you eh, manage to rent your place?

Dee   Rent it? *Sold* it!

Stef   Sol ... really? Wow.

Dee Yeah. Private treaty. Signed this morning. Builder bought it. Cash sale. Bang. Gone. I am *off* the property ladder.

Stef Oh …

Dee Yeah, and then I was thinking, shame Stef never saw the place, but then this builder guy said, 'Take the sale. Cut your losses. Don't put it on the market.'

Stef Really?

Dee Yeah. Fire damage. No one wants to know.

Stef Fire dam … how?

Dee Haven't a bull's. Least this way I don't have to worry if it was me. Em … drink?

Stef D … drink. Drink, drink, drink. Let's have a drink. Let's have a nice big Old Fashioned drink.

Stef *pours two drinks and hands one to* **Dee**.

Dee *clinks* **Stef**'s *glass.*

Dee Here's to us. Here's to knowing when you know.

Stef Yip.

They drink. **Stef** *nearly downs hers.* **Dee** *takes the glass out of her hand.*

Dee Ah- ah. Gimme that glass. I don't want you totally wasted. Not if you want to bang my brains out right now this very minute.

Dee *walks towards* **Stef** *with intent.*

Stef Just a … just a tick.

Stef *backs away and drinks.* **Dee** *gestures to the purple chair.*

Dee Want to sit down?

Stef No, no, no. I like … I like … up. I like standing up.

—

No, I was just thinking, the randomness of life, you know, what you were saying about the people and the telephones and the sperm and the pizza. You and me … If either of us had …

Dee Swiped the other way I know. We'd never have met. But you did. And I did. Then up you came, out of my telephone. Then when you said I love you so, so soon, I was just like wow! This woman, this woman is

30 Furniture

just … like some kind of wow, boom, miracle. Like a … digital saint. Yep, I need to just go with this, no matter where it takes me.

Stef Ha … *you* said I love you.

Dee Huh?

Stef You said I love you first. You definitely said it first.
No, I remember 'cause, where was I … fuck, that's loud.

Turning music off.

No, that's right, because I was in the office and I was sort of doing my *don't ring me at work* voice, you know, not *saying* don't ring me at work, just you know dropping the hint and … before you hung up you said, *I love you too.* And I thought awe, that's … cute, you know … like you *thought* you heard it so you said it back …

Dee You said, *I love you.*

Stef No, no, I said, *I'll leave you.* You know like, *Gotta love you and leave you.* So that's probably where you picked up the *I love you,* bit. You must have gone, *Oh no.*

Dee No.

Stef No. Well, it was cute, that's all I'm saying. It was one of those moments after I met you and thought, ah … 's cute.

Dee Cute.

Stef Yeah, cute.

Dee You think I'm cute.

Stef Of course I think you're cute. You're like a total cute.

Dee My ex used to say that.

Stef Say what?

Dee *Awe, you're so cute.* And then I'd say, *No one wants to fuck a cutie.* And I was right.

They eye each other. Shit's getting real. **Dee**, *takes a drink and puts her glass down on the table.* **Stef** *gets a coaster, puts it under the glass.* **Dee** *tries to touch her but she pushes her hand away.*

Stef Can we jus … not … just … time out for a second, just gimme a minute, okay. Back off.

Time out.

She paces up and down the room, looks at the purple chair, paces up and down again.

Dee   Stef, you're freaking me out. What's going on?

Stef   Dee, I'm sorry but, I can't have sex with you with that thing in the room.

Dee   What thing?

Stef   That. That … thing! That chair, if you can call it a chair. It looks more like –

Dee   Like what?

Stef   It looks like the Michelin Man shot Barney the Dinosaur, skinned him and wore him like a dress.

Dee   Sorry?

Stef   Oh come on Dee! It's a joke, isn't it? Ha, ha, ha, ha. It's a joke. Please tell me it's a joke.

Dee   What? Why? What's a joke?

Stef   This is like a moving in gag or something, isn't it? You know, you were probably passing a skip, or one of those shops where they sell all that stuff belonging to dead old people with no taste. Or maybe it was in the window with a sign on it saying, *Decommissioned hospital chemo lounger.* I dunno, and you said, 'Oh, big fuck-off purple chair! This'll really freak her out. This'll be hilarious. She'll think it's like my prized possession. She is going to die. I can't wait to see her face. I can't wait to see the relief on her face when she realizes I was jo …'

Dee   You don't like my chair?

Stef   … king … It's your chair. It's your chair? Oh, my god it is your chair.

Dee   You don't like my chair.

Stef   If I was redecorating a Russian mafia strip club, yes, I'd love that chair. But I'm not. I am a grown up, sophisticated coaster using, Old Fashioned drinking adult woman who appreciates nice things.

Dee   So, you don't like my chair?

Stef   Dee, *no one* should like that chair. I mean, do you? Do you *like* that chair?

32   Furniture

Dee   I don't know ... I ... never thought about it before. It's very comfortable ...

Slow breathing.

Hm ... bit stressed now.

Stef   Look –

Dee   Feel a bit ... judged.

Stef   I'm not judging you. I'm being honest, and you're mistaking that for being mean but I'm not being mean, it's the honesty that's mean. But, look at this place. Look around you Dee. This entire apartment has been repurposed, remodelled, and meticulously preserved to a classical state of arrested decay. That out there is a restored Tasmanian teak kitchen counter. That's Charles and Ray Eames limited edition bespoke table. That's an original Eileen Gray E-1027 side table. That's a giant malignant tumour of a purple chair. One of these kids is doing his own thing. Can you spot him out?

Dee (*hurt*)   You said bring your stuff.

Stef   I know I said bring your stuff.

Dee   So here it is. You said bring it so I brought it. I don't care about the chair. I care about you. I am here because I care about you. I want to live with you because you're here.

Because you exist within these three little concrete boxes, I want to exist here too, not because of what's *in* them, not because of your spaceship lamps and your robot name side tables. God, if you lived under a bridge I'd –

Stef   Spaceship lamps? Robot tables? Oh, that's lovely.

Dee   It's your thoughts, your views and opinions that matter, everything else is just window dressing for your soul.

Stef   Thoughts and views? Okay, this is getting way too intense.

Dee   Way too intense? I'm not the one who doesn't want to bang my total brains out right now this very minute because I own a purple chair.

Stef   I do! I do! I do! It's just I feel ... I feel like 1987 threw up in my living room and it's putting me off.

Dee   Stef, I'm not attracted to you because you've a nice dining room table.

Play Two: La-Z-Boy   33

Stef You – you're not? You're not.

Dee No. I'm not.

Stef –

You don't like my furniture?

Dee I … don't like it or not like it, I don't *think* about your furniture.

Stef Okay, just to clarify the point. The first night you came back here, you weren't like, wow.

Dee About what?

Stef About the place!

Dee No. I wasn't like wow. I was like wow, when we –

Stef Okay, forget about the sex. What about the decor? I manifested all these design choices out of my own brain because I want to say something to people about the kind of person I am. I want to make an impression. I want my home to say, I am discerning, I have class, I have taste, I am worldly, I am educated …

Dee Educated?

Stef Educated, yes …

Dee Name the world's poorest country.

Stef Uh …

Dee Republic of Congo. How many islands in the Pacific Ocean?

Stef Oh, come on, no one knows tha –

Dee Between twenty to thirty thousand. How many sank last year due to global warming? Five. Who wrote 'Air on a G String'?

Stef Victoria's Secret.

Dee Nope. What's China's GDP?

Stef F … seven.

Dee Eleven point two trillion. Who is the president of Syria?

Stef Okay, so you've read the internet. Congratu-bloody-lations. More of a sports woman myself, actually. That's how I know my *left* from *right*. That's how I know how to catch a set of keys when

34   Furniture

they're thrown at me, not like some … stoned, vegan, tree-hugging octopus.

Dee   Sport, right. That where you learned to *dodge* a question? Maybe your worldly, educated decor might know who the president of Syria is.

She goes to the dining table, leans right over it and asks it.

Excuse me, table, who is the president of Syria? Don't know? Fair enough. At least the table has an excuse for not knowing because it lacks the facility to be cognisant of its own existence. Unlike you, who does, which is why you have no excuse for not knowing who the president of Syria is.

Stef   –

Actually, do you know what, let's not forget about the sex, 'cause here's the thing. You would not be standing here today with the keys to my door in your hand if my place was a dump because if my place was a dump, the first night you came back here the sex would never have happened.

Dee   Of course it would have.

Stef   Why?

Dee   Because I wanted to sleep with you, not your Tasmanian kitchen.

Stef   Okay. Fine. So when you came in, the first time you came in, first impressions, you wouldn't have cared if this place looked like a crack den, no?

Dee   Yes, I'd have cared if it looked like a crack den because I care about you not taking crack.

Stef   You'd only known me for two hours. How could you possibly have cared about me, let alone if I was a drug addict? And if you did, well, whoa, hold it right there 'cause that is super stab-you-in-the-shower psycho needy.

Dee   You know when you know.

Stef   No, you don't necessarily know when you know. I could have been a very tidy, high functioning crack addict with impeccable taste. Hell, it's only been a month, you don't know me, I could still be.

My point is if this apartment was a dump, you wouldn't have stayed. You would have gone to the bathroom and messaged a friend to call you in ten minutes and pretend your mother's been in a car accident. Like a normal person.

Play Two: La-Z-Boy   35

Dee   Would you?

Stef   Would I what?

Dee   Shoe on the other foot, yes or no. If you'd gone back to mine instead of me to yours, would you have stayed?

Stef   I can't answer that.

Dee   Why not? I did.

Stef   Because you've seen my place. I never saw your place. And I never will ever be able to see your place because you must have lit one of your own brain farts and burned it to the ground.

Dee   You want to see my place? I'll show you my place. This is me, right now, in my place.

Dee *moves around the purple chair and sits in it provocatively, holding* **Stef**'s *gaze.*

Dee   Stef? Is that you? Door's open, come on in.

Dee *pulls a lever popping her legs out into the recliner position.* **Stef** *takes a little stagger backwards and puts her hand to her mouth.*

Stef   Ahhhh! Oh, Jesus. You're a h …, you're a hippy, aren't you? But you dress so well.

Dee   My sister gives me all her castoffs. I donate the money I would have spent on clothes to fast fashion awareness.

Stef *stifles a little vomit gag.*

Stef   How did I not see? You're a dumpster foraging, carbon light-foot hippy. But I don't get it.

You're so hot.

Dee   And I don't match your furniture. How do you think I feel? You went online and surfed for someone to compliment your couch. You plucked me from a digital line up like a plumb from a tree. You … ordered me on the internet. You had me boxed, shipped and delivered. Oh God, I feel disgusting. I feel so eBayed.

Stef   Dee, Dee, I can't –

Dee   Be with me? You think I want to be with someone who doesn't know about the world, care about the world? Well, I've got news for you Stef. It's not a pyramid, it's a circle. We are all connected. Me, you, and the eight-year old from Bangladesh who makes ten cents a day sewing

36　Furniture

your knickers. Don't think for a minute because you got stuff, because
you order sushi on your i-Pad, you're the only one of the three of us
who's allowed to make any choices.

–

You know, I don't care about the chair. I couldn't care less about the
chair. I do care that your good or bad opinion of the ephemeral objects
surrounding my living presence exponentially affects your enjoyment *of*
my living presence. That, I do care about.

Stef　–

Meaning?

Dee　Meaning ten minutes ago I knocked on your door and you wanted
to bang me in front of the neighbours. Throw in a piece of furniture that
clashes with your Danish mid-century ...

Stef　Mid-century Danish!!

Dee　Mid-century fucking Danish table and you're all zipped up
quicker than a *nun* in a *blizzard*. Meaning the fact that you are physically
unable to make love to me when there's a purple chair in the room makes
you shallow.

Ergo, I am now physically unable to make love to you as it would be an
indictment on my good judge of character, on everything I value.

Stef　Meaning I'm too dumb to ... You think I'm stupid.

Dee　I didn't say you were stupid, I *inferred* that you were shallow.

Stef　You think stupid people are capable of possessing all this? Hm?
That. That. This. Five of them. One of those. These? You think stupid
people have these?

Stef *opens a jar, scoops up two fistfuls of Nespresso pods and lets them rain through
her fingers. (The gold-coloured ones work best.)*

Stef　Well, here's the news in four easy peel words Dee. Smart. Folk.
Get. Stuff.

Dee　And here's the news for you Stef. You know how long the pleasure
centres of your brain remain stimulated for after making a material
purchase? Ninety days. That's all you get. – *Oh that's a nice lamp.* Tick, tick,
tic. Ninety days. Boom. You're depressed. You feel empty but you don't
know why, so you think. – *I know, I'll buy a magazine rack for my collection of*

articles about how to suck the fat out of my ass and inject it in my face, ah, I'm happy again. Tick, tick, tick. – *Is it just me or is life pointless? Oh, look, plates designed by that gastro-pornographer wanker telly chef. Ah, those plates feel so nice.* – Tick, tick, tick. – *God I hate myself. Oh, look the toaster's broken. Cool, this one's got lots of buttons on it that don't really do anything.* – Tick, tick, tick. – *Oh, dear, it clashes with the kitchen. It makes want to kill myself. I know! I'll get a new kitchen –*

Stef *grabs a sofa cushion and squashes it into* **Dee**'*s face.*

Stef   Stop! Stop it! Stop it right now. Shut up! Just shut up! Jus … Shut. Up. Stop … jus … jus … stop talking. I'm tired. I want to be …. Alone. I want to be alone in a room with no one in it. An … an … an … with no … things I … don't like.

Cushion slips from her hands.

I want straight lines and crisp pleats and smooth surfaces, and flawless, unsplashed backsplashes, and chrome that has never known a fingerprint, and coffee-ringless coffee tables and, and, and boutique teak and the cool, clean feel of exemplary upholstery.

And I try, I try … but people … people … I see people everywhere with people in bars and parks and train stations, kissing, touching, holding, linking thoughts through each other's eyes, and doing that thing with the hair where you push it behind the other person's ear and I think, yes. Me. That. Here. But then …

She runs a hand over the spot on the table where the keys landed.

–

Dee …

Dee   I know.

Stef   I'm going to have to let you go.

Dee   Where? Me and my chair, where are we to go?

Stef   Oh. You can take the bed. I'll sleep out here. We can work this out tomorrow.

Dee   It's okay. You take the bedroom. I'll sleep out here on this.

Stef   Come on, Dee, you can't sleep all night in that chair.

Dee   Why not? Why do you think we never went to mine?

Stef   I'll get you a blanket.

38   Furniture

She goes to the closet, opens the door. Twenty Lidl bags tumble out at her feet. She is gray with revulsion.

Actually, tell you what, you stay here tonight. I'm going to get a hotel.

Dee   You don't have to do that.

Stef   A month!

Picks up Nespresso pods.

What was I thinking? Who was I thinking I was?

Picks up another Nespresso pod.

Who was I thinking we were?

Stef *looks at the Nespresso pods in a state of vulnerable confusion.*

I wanted this I know I did. I must have done. I bought new sheets.

– Stay. I'll come back tomorrow. I'll make everything okay. I'll … pay for … something to happen … tomorrow.

Dee   If that's what you know you want, well, then you should probably go.

Stef   Yes. You know when you know.

Dee   Tomorrow then.

Stef   Tomorrow.

Dee   Stef?

Stef   Dee?

Dee   Your soul is not your sofa.

Stef *exits.*

Dee *sits in the purple La-Z-Boy, staring into space. She takes out a roll-up out of a tobacco tin and lights it.*

She picks up a remote and points it towards the stereo. On comes 'Buttons and Bows' sung by Dinah Shore. She smokes and listens to the music.

After a few drags, her eyes start to close. Her cigarette hand droops over the magazine rack as she falls asleep. An ASM in white gloves enters and wheels her away.

Play Three

Chaise Longue

The lights fade up on a council flat.

Various high queer aesthetic furniture clutters the room, including a chaise longue, which can only be described as a parody of luxury that time has rendered obsolete.

Michael *is by a record player, looking through a record collection. He is wearing an old London Irish rugby jersey. If he wears glasses, they'd be two-for-one at Specsavers. His trousers look like they were bought by his wife in a hurry. He's been up too long, the limits of his diplomatic skills wearing thin at the edges.*

George *lies in high blankets on a hospital type chair. Opposite is an elaborate chaise longue. He is wearing colourful silk pyjamas and a dressing gown. There is a table with medications, a bed urinal and a box of tissues. He is very weak but agitated and peppery: no response is acceptable and no gesture of help is sufficient.*

As **Michael** *flips through the records,* **George** *pops his tablets, watching him.*

George   That's not Julie Andrews.

Michael   I know it's not Julie Andrews, George.

George   That's Dinah Shore.

Michael   I know.

George   Dinah –

Michael   I know it's not Julie Andrews but Julie Andrews isn't here.

George   Turn. Her. Off.

Michael *turns off Dinah Shore.*

George   Now look again.

Michael   Julie Andrews isn't there, I'm telling you.

George   Christ's sake, Michael, she *is* there.

Michael   George, I've looked twice, she's *not* there.

George *(taking a packet of gummy bears out of his pocket)*   Are you *absolutely* sure?

Michael   Positively sure.

George   Look again.

40   Furniture

Michael   If I look again, will you let me get on with everything else?

George (*considers this*)   Yes.

Pops a gummy bear.

Michael   Promise.

George   Promise.

Michael   'Cause I *have* to go soon.

George   So you keep saying.

Pops another gummy bear.

Michael   Right. Cats, Chess, Funny Girl, Forty Second Street, Phantom Of The Opera, Sweet Charity, Tell Me On A Sunday, West Side Story, The Wizard Of Oz –

George (*snapping*)   That's W! You've gone past it.

Michael   George!

George   M. M. M. She's under M!

Michael   There's no My Fair Lady in here.

George   Sure?

Michael   Yes!

He sits on the chaise longue. He turns his attention to a shoe box of unruly papers.

George   Balls. I wanted Julie to see me out. That camp has a row of tents, Grindr reject, girl guide effort of a fairy nurse must have nicked it. Bloody twinkies. Like jackdaws so they are. Never trust hired help who offers to tidy. That one was always trying to *have a bit of a tidy*. My own fault for telling him it was signed. Bloody eyes. Can't see what they're stuffing down their pants. Most likely strolled out of here with my Mary Poppins salt and pepper shakers stuck up his ass. Ow …

Michael   Ow?

George   Ow. Ow. Ow …

Michael   Are you sure you don't have them stuck up yours?

George   Fuck off.

(*Breathless.*)   Ow!

Michael   Where?

Play Three: Chaise Longue   41

Michael *puts down the box.*

George   Ow … my back.

Michael   You want a pillow?

George   No.

Michael   Here.

George   Get off.

Michael   Pillow here.

George   I can't! It doesn't go with my pyjamas.

—

Sing us a song, would you?

Michael   No.

George   Sing us a song to see me out.

Michael   You're not *going* out.

George (*singing*)

I could have danced all night … da da …. Yah da di da da.

—

'Mom. Do that one.

Michael   I don't know it.

George   Course you do.

Michael   I don't know it any*more*.

Michael *sorts him with difficulty and fussing.*

George   You were marvellous in that. Who played Eliza?

Michael   Have some water.

George   Whoever it was, she'd the wrong shape face for that hat. She looked like Phillip Treacy sat on a marrow.

Michael   She was eleven.

George   No excuse.

Michael   Drink.

42   Furniture

George   Yes, I'll have a pink martini with a maraschino cherry, extra dry.

Michael   Water, here. Drink.

George   I'm not a plant.

Michael   Drink.

George *takes a sip.*

George   Ugh. Where's my sweets?

Michael (*finding them*)   Here.

George   What?

Michael (*placing them in* **George**'s *hand*)   They'll rot your teeth.

George   Piss off.

He pops a gummy bear. **Michael** *goes to the box of papers and sifts through the contents.*

Michael   Right, let's get through this.

George *takes the bed urinal and puts it to his ear like a telephone.*

George   Hello, Julie. George calling Julie. Come in Julie dear. Come and sing an old queen an old song would you? My crown is slipping.

Michael   I'm taking your lease agreement with me, okay?

George (*to* **Michael**)   Darling, it's yours.

(*Singing*)

Ya da da di da da. Danced all night … 'Mom.

Michael   I'll take these utilities as well.

George   Ya da da da di da.

Michael   Did you hear me, George?

George   Ugh! *You* should have stuck with singing, you loon. Instead of … What's it you do?

Michael   Solicitor.

George   Solicitor. Well la di da. Christ, what a waste.

(*To urinal phone.*) Julie!

Play Three: Chaise Longue   43

Michael *is esxasperated at* **George***'s refusal to listen. He puts down the shoe box and finds his pad and pencil.*

Michael   Right then, your personal effects. Let's start with the couch.

George (*disgusted*)   Chaise longue, if you don't mind.

Michael   The chaise long.

George   Chaise lon*gue*. Get it right.

Michael   Chaise long.

George   Long -guh.

Michael   Long -guh.

George   Uh!

Michael   Uh.

George   Couch. As if.

Returning to urinal phone.

Michael   Where do you want it to go?

George (*to urinal phone*)   Julie darling!

Michael   George, get off the phone.

George   Yes poppet, he's here!

Michael   We need to sort the furniture.

George   Yes, Julie, he arrived this morning with his pad and pencil poised to collate my chattels. Want anything chicken? I've a lovely little nest of tables I named after the Von Trapps. – Brigetta, Liesel and Kurt. You want them? – Oh, it's no trouble. What's your address?

Michael   We need to sort where it's all going.

George   I'm doing it!

(*To* **Julie**.)   Yes, Julie poppet, my secondaries have secondaries, so I'm afraid the queen of Tower Hamlets is leaving the building.

Michael   The chaise longue. Where do you wan –

George (*to* **Julie**)   No darling, he *can't* stay, he's off tonight, back to ticky tacky Lego land.

Michael   Where would you like it to go?

44   Furniture

George   *Sorry Julie? Is* he in the West End? Well I'm glad you asked. No. He chucked it all in and became a solicitor. – Well, I blame his father for telling him singing was for poofs. Had him down the rugby club faster than shit off a shovel. Farewell Freddie Ernsford-Hill. – No, sadly not, he … ha, ha, ha … he only went and hitched himself up to a paloneomi – Hm – hatched her a couple feeles and everything. Naff little eeks on them.

Michael   George!

George   What are you saying to me, Michael?

Michael (*like **George** is deaf*)   The chaise longue. *Where* do you *want* it to *go*?

George   Oh …

–

(*Impatient.*)   Well, did you *call* the good people in Knightsbridge?

Michael   Yes.

George   And?

Michael   The V&A politely declined.

George   And the MET.

Michael   No.

George   What about Les Girls in Sydney?

Michael   They closed in 1994.

George   Well, I can't say I didn't see that coming. Big hairy lallies on them.

Michael   So our other options are –

He refers to his notepad.

George   Bunch of fat bushmen in bouffants. Drag Queens? Dragged though a hedge moreaslike.

Michael (*referring to notes*)   I looked up Phillip Walton.

George   Good, he's a big collector.

Michael   He has dementia. He doesn't remember.

George   What about Julian Park?

Play Three: Chaise Longue   45

Michael   He died a year ago.

George   Ah. So you've been through my little book.

–

Well, who's alive?

Michael   Roger White.

George   Rancid little cock. No way.

Michael   Okay.

George   After what he did to me? Over my dead body.

Michael   Emma Stanhope.

George   That lumpy old dyke? She'll chop it into firewood.

Michael   Peter Dean.

George   Oh, Peter Dean! Perfect! Send the chaise longue to him.

Michael   He's in Canada.

George   That's nice.

Michael   It'll cost nine hundred to ship.

Pause. **George** *fixes his dressing gown, pops a gummy bear.*

George   Is there no one else?

Michael *glues his eyes to his notebook. It's coming, he knows it.*

George (*with performed surrender*)   Well, that's it. *You* win. I leave the chaise longue – to you.

Michael   George I –

George   No honestly, don't thank me chicken, I *know* it's why you came. Besides, I've *seen* your house. It's the *least* I can do.

Michael   It's just ... I ... I ... I ...

George   Aye, aye captain, what?

Michael   I ... don't know what to say.

George   Well, try *thank you* for starters.

Michael   I can't.

George   Nonsense. Don't be silly.

46 Furniture

Michael No –

George Up you suddenly pop after nigh on a decade? *Oh, no I can't!* Well, pull the other one with the ring-a-dings on it would you, dicky bow. I see right through your little scheme.

Michael George no –

George I mean it's part of your childhood, isn't it? Makes sense you'd *want* to have it. The legacy. It's only fair, you'd want it, for the connection. To *me*.

Michael (*under breath*) Oh god –

George That's settled, the chaise longue is yours. *Oh, no I can't!* Why else would you be here?

Michael The home care people called.

George Bugger the home care people.

Michael It's time. We have to get things in order.

George I've changed my mind, I'm not going in.

Michael But it's all arranged.

George (*getting antsy*) Oh, shush, no more of it. Chattels done. Now, there's a catalogue *some*where. Where did I put it?

Michael I –

George I *need* to show you the urn I want.

Michael I'm just here to help you –

George *pulls a catalogue from under him and flicks through it.*

George I had it marked, where the blazes is it …

Michael (*looking at chaise longue, panic rising*) We've no room.

George *finds the item and shows* **Michael**.

George Now pay attention and don't mess this up, I'm thinking Greek amphora in fuschia with a semi-opaque glaze.

Michael I could maybe take some small things, jewellery for the girls but –

George Look here. Classy isn't it? That will be lovely up on your mantlepiece – if you can spare the room with *her* golfing bollox.

Play Three: Chaise Longue   47

Michael (*with more punch than intended*)   We've nowhere to put it, George!

George *looks at* **Michael** *with the quizzical hurt expression of a disappointed child.*

George   Oh.

–

You … can't take it?

Michael   I can't take it. The urn, of course I can take. Of course. But the sofa –

George   Chaise longue.

Michael   Chaise longue.

–

No.

George   No?

Michael   I can't.

George   No, you can't *take* it …

–

Or no, you don't *want* it?

Michael   Oh, no …

George   Well, which is it?

Michael   George I –

George   Well? Do you want it or not want it?

Michael (*getting up and looking at the chaise longue*)   I do, I do, I do.

George   Then take it.

Michael   I can't.

George   Why not?

Michael   I … I want it. Okay. I w … It's not that I don't *want* it, it's just I –

George   Just. Just. Just. I. I. I. Spit it out would you, you sound like a sea lion with a stroke.

48   Furniture

Michael   We've things of our own now. Barbara … and I. Things we've picked, for *our* home that are special to *us*. And with the girls being small, you have to have a more … utilitarian approach to the things around you.

So we've no … I would have loved to have taken it but it's not *me* any more – I mean it's not *just* me anymore and I'm not sure how it would all … blend … with what we have …

George   I see.

Michael   Oh, good.

George   I see exactly who's behind this.

Michael   Oh, now Barb –

George   It's her isn't it?

Michael   Barb –

George   That flat-shoed, club swinging Yeti.

Michael   Barb –

George   She's gone and nipped off your gonads and teed them off for a hole in one, hasn't she?

Michael   It's *not* Barbara, George. And while we're at it, I can't have –

George   Ow …

Michael   I can't –

George   Ow, ow, ow.

Michael   I can't have you –

George   Oh god the pain! Ah, ah, ah …

Michael *watches the display of agony with firm resistance to the drama, then softens.*

Michael   Where?

George   In my broken heart, you little prick!

Michael   George. No soap opera, please.

Breath, start over.

Barbara and I are –

Play Three: Chaise Longue   49

George   Ow –

Michael   We like to make our decisions as a family.

George   Oh god the pain.

George, *with the bag of gummy bears, munches one.*

Michael   *Particularly* when it comes to the house.

George   Ah …

Michael   Barb – Would you please stop stuffing your face with sweets while I am trying to talk to you!

George   These are not sweets, you fucktard! It's medical marijuana. That home help clepto-fag sneaks it in from California.

Michael   Well stop.

George (*popping another*)   No, I'm getting off my face, I can't bear to listen to you.

Michael   That's enough!

George   *That's enough.* What ever happened to your lovely lisp? You sound like you're talking through a side of beef. And look at you. Look at you! With your *hideous* shoes and your *biscuit*-coloured trousers and your … this! Whatever the … rugger buggery fuck this is.

Where's Barbie, Ken?

Michael   George.

George   Know what you are, nephew dear?

Michael   I know who I am.

George   You –

Minister   I know who I am and I like who I am.

George   You are the tragedy I shall take to my grave.

Michael   George, you'll kill yourself.

George (*getting upset*)   Good! Because I'll tell you what, ducky. I am not going into that place so you can forget about that for starters. I am staying here. I'm going to pop *My Fair Lady* on the player, there's a bottle of fizz in the fridge and it's going down the hatch with a fistful of mogadons and the rest of these and that's it. Me and Julie are off on a cloud of bubbles. And as for you? Breezing in at the eleventh hour after

50   Furniture

God knows how long, telling *me* what to do with *my* belongings. Well I'm not going anywhere and you can't make me go. My last glimmer of the world should be of the things I know. Not some fluorescent, wipe-down ... fucking ...

Michael   They're good people.

George   No good person makes you wear crocs!

Michael (*starting to wobble but holds it steady*)   Look, just

(*sitting*)

I know this is hard and that's why I'm here. And I'm sorry. Right, I'm sorry about things and I'm sure you're sorry about things but I'm here to help. I'm here to help you now. And I know this is hard ... But I'm all you've got so can we please just bite the bit and get real with this for a minute?

George   Real? Get real? This is a highly sought-after collectable artifact. This chaise longue came right out of Danny La Rue's dressing room at the Palace Theatre. Barbra Streisand sat on it. Rudolph Nureyev sat on it. Noel Coward, *Princess Margaret* sat on it. Judy Garland *passed out* on it. It's made of Belizean mahogany, stuffed with Tuscan crimped horsehair and it is a priceless fucking museum piece. So. You. Get. Real.

We hear a tick, tick, tick and the sound of a coin dropping into a cash tray. The lights go out.

Michael *lights a candle. He goes outside. We hear coins being fed into a meter. The lights come on.* **Michael** *returns, sits.*

Michael   Can I get you anything?

George   I'd like a time machine that goes to 1967.

—

Stay.

Michael   I have to get back.

George   I won't be long, I promise –

Michael   School starts tomorrow. I need to be there for the photo.

George   Or your lady of Lesbos will go through the roof.

Michael   My wife isn't a lesbian George.

Play Three: Chaise Longue   51

George   No? Well her hair is. That wedding picture you sent. Christ on a bike. Ha! She looked like Quasimodo got punched in the face and fell in a box of meringues. Ha. Ha. Ha. Ha. Ha.

Michael (*waits for the laughter to fade*)   George, I love you very much. I love you as a son loves any parent. In many ways you taught me things my own parents couldn't see I needed. You taught me that a bully is more scared of you than you are of him, because you like yourself and he hates you for that. You taught me the sharpest weapon in a fight is the tongue in your head. And if that doesn't work, the quickest exit is your legs. Because of you I knew there were laws in our own country that made criminals out of innocent people. And that's why you went away. And that was unjust. And if I wanted to change it, for my own children, I should do something about it. So I studied law.

—

You taught me how to sing at a party: Never say yes straight away, always make them wait. You taught me how to iron a shirt, fix the hem of a skirt, ice a birthday cake. And most importantly, you taught me that you don't need a soldier's uniform to be brave, for courage has a most extensive wardrobe. Because you were never afraid to be you, I have never been afraid to be me and for that I can never forget you.

—

But if you speak about my wife like that again, that will be all I remember you for. If you speak about how she looks, what she wears, or how she chooses to decorate our home, I will get my things and go. And leave you to wonder why I don't *want* your sofa, George. Why would I want to inherit your furniture, if that's how it reminds me of you? Clear? Are we clear, George? Blink if you're too proud to answer. I need to know before I go.

A pause. **George** *blinks.*

George   —

You were the funniest little boy. Ha … Never liked anything matching. Used to come in here and pull everything out of the wardrobe. You'd dress up like a basket of fruit.

Gesturing to chaise longue.

You'd climb up on that old thing and do all the classics. *The King and I. Mary Poppins. My Fair Lady.* Ha! *Some Like It Hot.* Ha, you, were, terrific.

52   Furniture

Michael   Osgood, I can't get married in your mother's dress ... She and I, we're not built the same way.

George   We can have it altered.

Michael   Osgood, I'm going to level with you, we can't get married at all.

George   Why not?

Michael   In the first place, I'm not a natural blonde.

George   I don't care.

Michael   I smoke, I smoke all the time.

George   I don't care.

Michael   Well I've a terrible past. For three years now I've been living with a saxophone player.

George   I forgive you.

Michael   Ah, you don't understand Osgood. I'm a man!

George   Well ...

George/Michael   Nobody's perfect! Bum-ba-bum-ba-bum-ba-bum ... ba-bum!

George   How old, your two?

Michael   Five and seven.

Michael *realizes it's his chance to show* **George** *a picture. He places his phone it in* **George***'s hand and scrolls through the photos for him.*

Michael   That's Kate. She does martial arts. Won't take off the uniform, even in bed. That's he with the Barbie doll she got for her birthday. She calls it Kevin. That's Mary in the pink. Everything has to be pink or there's war.

Looks at the chaise longue, looks away.

There's Barbara at the barbecue. The girls love that. 'Cause Barbara and barbecue ...

When you're small, rhymes are like miracles. And that's me there ... giving the garden furniture a wipe after the rain.

George   How old?

Play Three: Chaise Longue   53

Michael   Five and seven.

George   Bring me Josephine.

Michael *picks up a foot stool and gives it to* **George**, *who lifts the lid and gingerly picks through the jewellery inside.*

George   Who's eleven?

Michael   Seven. Kate is seven.

George *glances at the photo again and picks out an item of jewellery.*

George   That's for her. And who is five?

Michael   Mary.

George   Here, she is to have this one.

—

Don't mix them up.

George *places the jewellery in* **Michael**'s *hand.*

Their hands remain clasped for a moment.

Michael   G ...

George   Shush ... Ow.

Michael   Ow?

George   Ow.

Michael   Where?

George   Life. Life is oh so very sore.

—

Dauphin, dauphin, I had such plans for you.

Looks about the room, takes it all in.

Look at all this stuff. There is so much stuff in the world that has nowhere to go. We spend our lives collecting this from here and that from there. Little birds with twigs and leaves. Then one day it's as if all the floors and ceilings and walls start to tick. And all our things, our encumbrance of mementos that have stayed stock still for so long, the benchmarks of our lives, begin to tremor and shake. Then ... pish, it all blows apart like a firework. It all just flies away like it never knew you. Off they go, all the little pieces of your life, into trucks and car boots. And they don't

54   Furniture

remember. The rug doesn't remember the dancing. The tables don't remember the food. The wardrobe doesn't remember the gowns. Away you slip and off they fly, all your formica memories, to set the scene in someone else's life. Furniture is not sentimental. You can love it but it won't remember who you are.

George*'s gummy bears hit his system.*

George   Whoah.

—

Stoned, looks at gummy bear bag.

– I. Am. Completely. Off. My. Face.

—

Sing us a song, would you?

Michael *does his best Julie Andrews.*

Michael   George? Geor ... ge.

George   Hm ... who's there?

Michael   It's Julie, George.

George   Julie, darling, is that really you?

Michael   Yes, George.

George   Julie, I'm doing my list. Would you like my chaise longue from Danny La Rue's ... palace dressing room ...?

Michael *(noticing something by the record player)*   Yes, George, I'd like that very much.

George   My nephew has a pen and pencil. He'll put you down. So many things ... I don't know what's to be done.

Michael   Don't worry. Michael will look after everything for you.

George   Oh good. He is such a good boy.

Michael   Yes.

George   Do you know, he's taking *all* the furniture.

Michael *(approaches record player)*   *Yes*, he's taking *all* the furniture.

He picks up Julie Andrews record.

Play Three: Chaise Longue   55

George   Julie, do you know, Michael couldn't find you.

Michael (*putting on record*)   That's all right. He found me in the end.

George   Tired now ...

Julie Andrews   Bed, bed, I couldn't go to bed,

My head's too light to try to set it down,

Michael *joins in. As the song builds momentum, he grows into the performance until his is in full West End mode.* **George** *conducts gleefully.*

Julie/Michael   Sleep, sleep I couldn't sleep tonight.

Not for all the jewels in the crown.

I could have danced all night, I could have danced all night,

And still have begged for more,

Walking to the chaise longue.

I could have spread my wings and done a thousand things

I've never done before

I'll never know what made it so exciting

Getting up on the chaise longue.

Why all at once my heart took flight

I only know when he began to dance with me

I could have danced, danced, danced all night.

We hear a tick, tick, tick and a coin falling into a cash drawer. The lights go out to the very last beat of the song.

Once Upon a Bridge

The world premiere of *Once Upon a Bridge* was live streamed from Druid's The Mick Lally Theatre in Galway on 11 February 2021. Following an initial run of four live stream performances to homes in Ireland and 35 countries around the world, the play was then made available for on demand viewing for a further four days that same month.

'compelling ... delicately uplifting' The Guardian
'packs a terrific, touching punch' Sunday Independent
'a fascinating new drama' The Irish Times

2021 World Premiere Company

Cast

A Woman	Siobhán Cullen
The Bus Driver	Adetomiwa Edun
A Man	Aaron Monaghan

Creative Team

Writer	Sonya Kelly
Director	Sara Joyce
Lighting & Set Design	Sinéad McKenna
Sound Design & Composition	Alma Kelliher
Movement	David Bolger
Costume Design	Clíodhna Hallissey
Assistant Director	Emily Foran

Once Upon a Bridge

For bus drivers everywhere

Cast of characters

A Man, *a white male in his mid-thirties, British accent. He wears trousers, a smart shirt, no tie, and leather shoes.*

The Bus Driver, *a black male in his thirties/forties. His accent is a mix of African and European with notes of London. He wears a bus driver's uniform.*

A Woman, *a white female in her early thirties. Her accent is west of Ireland which flips effortlessly to English. She wears a smart black knee-length coat and skirt (not too restrictive, pockets are good) with a white shirt, and flat black shoes.*

Script note

Italics in dialogue indicate the character is performing the voice of someone or speaking directly to a person in their story.

A double space between lines suggests a beat, breath, change in energy or a new thought.

An empty stage.

A projection screen looms somewhere over head height, perhaps not too conspicuously.

A spot of light appears. **A Man** *steps into it and addresses the audience directly. His tone is calm, confiding, contemplative – tender even. No sharp edges or sudden moves.*

A Man
In the McDonald's on the high street opposite my flat, They used to
have a lot of trouble at night,
With antisocial behaviour.

Drug deals,
Drug use,
Fist fights,
Knife fights,
Bottle fights,
Racist abuse,
Sexual assault,
Arson,
Petty theft.
Minor acts of crime
Largely brought on by a combination
Of cider and disappointment.

So they do this thing now
Around the time the pubs let out.

They play classical music.

Apparently,
It is scientifically proven to quell the rage,
And stymie the hunger to howl at the moon.
I look over there now,
Friday night,
Two in the morning,
They're quiet as church mice,
Sipping Cokes and munching fries to the sound of *Clair
     de Lune.*

One night,
I was standing at the window,
When this young lad swaggers in,
Tight cut shirt,
Skinny jeans,

62 Once Upon a Bridge

Peaky Blinder haircut –
You can tell by the walk
That he's scanning for prey.
So as he's headed to the counter,
He sort of clips this guy with his shoulder as he walks the
  other way.
They stop,
Stare each other down,
Size each other up,
Flex their necks,
Ball their fists
And take their stand.

We hear the distant sound of Clair de Lune.

And I'm thinking,
Uh-oh, here we go.

But then I see the music land.

Next thing you know
One of them bows,
The other one curtsies,
And off they go,
Hand in hand,
Waltzing in and out between the tables like a white tie ball,
One – two – three,
One – two – three,
One – two – three.
I watched them for a while and I have to say,
From far away,
It was quite beautiful to look at.

I think about that now,
When I think about her,
And what happened on the bridge.

Another spot of light opens up. **The Bus Driver** *steps into it as
the music fades. His energy is similar to* **A Man***: easy, calm, confiding ...*

The Bus Driver
It's Friday morning,
5th of May,
In the year of 2017,
My alarm goes off at 3 am.

Once Upon a Bridge   63

I wash,
Dress,
Fill my flask and lift my keys.
Silent as a samurai,
So as not to disturb my wife sleeping on the sofa.
Her weekday shift finishes at eleven.
She gets home at twelve,
Then she's up at six again to get the girls to school.
I start work at five,
So we have a separate sleeping system until the weekend.
So we get a proper rest
And I'm not tired at the wheel.
It's not ideal,
But what is in life
I suppose?

We don't have a car here yet.
Next year we will –
Just need to save a little more.
So I walk sixty-five minutes from our home to Putney
    Garage in the dark.
On the high street,
Up ahead,
A group of lads wearing traffic cones for hats,
Fall against parked cars to set off their alarms.
I cross the road to pass them by,
As clearly they're not finished with the evening's
    entertainment
And I have no desire to become the cherry on their cake.

At 4:30 am,
I clock in for work.
The locker room is silent:
Just a muffled hush
Of coats and bags being stored away.
There is,
As a rule,
Never any chatter in the morning.

Our supervisor knocks on the door.
Chop, chop you lot!
Get your backsides moving.

64   Once Upon a Bridge

You can tell by his tone
That the stress of his job
Has robbed him of his manners.

I want to see perfect runs today,
Or you'll be hearing from me,
You know who you are.

Recently,
The powers that be
Have been having a lot of trouble with the early shift:
A few 'bad apples'
If you get my drift,
Not sticking to the schedule.

Every bus driver must at all times
Do their very best to achieve a perfect run:
Depart on the dot,
Return on the dot,
Hitting every stop along the route
According to the timetable.
But in a city like London,
With all the chaos of trucks,
Traffic jams,
Road works,
And pedestrians not looking where they're going,
It is almost impossible to achieve this golden standard.
But still,
Those powers that be,
They track you on the GPS,
Watching all the while.
And if they don't like what they see,
Well …
You know who you are.

'Bad apples …'

He scans the room
Sizing up his weary battalion
Of London Transport workers.
Shifting his gaze,
From one to the next,
Until finally he lands his eyes on me,

As if to ask,
Are you the piece of rotten fruit I can decide to throw away?

Something clicks inside his head. Now he has something to prove.

So I quickly put away my things,
And head down to the depot,
Thinking just you wait my friend,
You don't know *who* I am,
You don't know *where* I've been,
You don't know *what* I've seen.
But today is the day you're going to see
That rotten apple is not *me*,
Because this morning for your viewing pleasure,
'Mister Supervisor'

I am going to execute the perfect run.

At 4:50 I step on the bus for safety checks:
Lights,
Brakes,
Indicators,
Mirrors,
Bells,
Doors,
All in working order.

4:55 am,
I lead the caravan of buses,
Ready for the signal.
Through the garage doors I see
A lemon wedge of light has popped into the sky.
It's going to be a sunny day.
I adjust my blinds
And at 4:59 the whistle blows.
Then:
Signal,
Mirror,
Lights,
Engine on,
And three,
Two,
One,
At 5:00 am

66   Once Upon a Bridge

Exactly to the second,
Bus four three zero rolls away.

Another spot of light opens. **A Woman** *steps in between the men as the music fades.*

A Woman
When I was small,
I would sit on my grandmother's knee,
And ask,
Granny, what happened to your nose?
And she'd reply,
Once upon a time,
The fairies had a dance
And asked me could they use it for a ballroom.

My Gran and Grandad moved from Connemara
To London in the nineteen-fifties to seek their fortunes.
He was a builder,
And she a dressmaker
With notions of working
In one of those posh lady's fashion houses.
She could turn a sheep's bladder into a ball gown,
She was that good with a needle.
Not even the signs along the Kilburn Road –
No Blacks.
No Dogs.
No Irish –
Bothered her a bit,
English being her second language.
Besides,
They mean those porter guzzling Jackeen thugs,
Who swear and beat their wives.
Not *her* class of people.

One morning,
Rush hour so it was,
On her way to Regent Street for an interview at a dress
    shop,
She's ascending the stairs at Piccadilly station,
When all at once
A briefcase and bowler hat
Lands upon her from the other way.
She hardly has the time to think which side is best to
    move,

When the icy lance of his umbrella
Catches sharp between her thighs.
She loses her footing,
And down she tumbles.
One full flight of cold hard stairs,
Bone on brass,
Brass on bone,
Down and down
Back into the belly of the Underground –
To her dying day she swears it was on purpose.
For no *Sorry madam*,
Did she hear.
No *Can I help you?* neither.
Just two words spat
From under his waxed moustache,
As he stepped across her body:

Keep.
Left.

And as the spank of his leather soles
Disappeared into the tunnel,
She cried alone to herself as Gaeilge,
Ceard a rinne mé?
Ceard a rinne mé?
Ceard a rinne mé?

She was pregnant at the time,
With dad.
So she fought the natural reflex to use her hands to
    protect herself,
Holding them across her middle to protect my father
    instead.
The fall destroyed her face.
Broke her nose.
Teeth.
Cheekbone.
Lost her sense of smell.
She arrives at Regent Street
Half an hour late.
Black and blue,
Blood all down her brand new coat
Teeth inside her pocket.

68   Once Upon a Bridge

They take one look at her,
And she knows just what they're thinking.
No, she says, *No!*
My husband's not been drinking.
I'm after being given shove,
She says,
I'm after having a fall.
But the closing door does not stall to listen
To her case.
Instead it creaks
And swings,
Then slams itself across her swollen face,
And she is left,
Bereft,
With no fair hearing.

She went back to Ireland to …
'Have the baby at home',
And never returned to London city.
A fair excuse,
For having the confidence knocked out of her,
Literally.

When I learned the truth about her nose,
And I asked my Gran what happened to the nasty man,
She simply said,
Learn this loveen,
And don't forget it:
Not all bad men go to prison.

And it's funny to think of me,
Living in London now,
Walking up those very same steps at Piccadilly station,
That if all those years ago,
She'd just told a lazy lie and said,
Yes loveen,
The man was put away,

I probably wouldn't have become a barrister today.

A Man

I met my wife at a wedding.
Got a tip off from the groom that morning.
Friend of the bride,

American lawyer,
Absolute ten,
Amazing body,
Gorgeous face,
Over here working on some international criminal case.
So he scribbles her name on my hand,
And when the band strikes up that night I look for ...

He reads the name on his hand.

Em ... il ... y ...

He looks up and is immediately transfixed by ...

Only to see that Emily is not a ten.
Emily is ...
Beau ... ti ... ful ...
In a way true beauty has no number.
Did you ever look across a crowded room
Only to be met with a vision of your future life?
Yeah, well it was that.
Garden.
Children.
Birthday clowns.
Holidays in France.
I could literally *see* our dinnerware,
Elegant,
Shining,
Like her hair ...
I swear there couldn't be a man alive
Who wouldn't want her for his wife.

So I do my best to catch her eye,
Which is not easy,
Because she's talking to this guy,
Some lanky,
Boney faced accountant
In a borrowed suit called '*Wayne*',
And she's all caught up in his fishing line
Of gangly arms and elbows.
And I can see the groom is looking on,
Laughing at me –
Prick –
Not having that,

70   Once Upon a Bridge

No way.
So I take my pint,
And as I approach,
A nifty 'accidental' bump followed by a …
Sorry mate!
Relegates *Wayne* to the lavatory
With a massive lager stain.
And then I turn to Emily and say,

He flips demeanour and becomes effortlessly charming.

Ahem.
Pardon me,
I may not be the best looking guy here,
But I am the best man,
And I wonder,
If I may have the honour of this dance?
And she goes,
Well how nice of you to ask.
And I go,
Well I am a gentleman.
And she says – And *this* is what got me – She says,
Well, if you're a gentleman,
You'll know the first rule of being a gentleman is
A gentleman never calls himself a gentleman.
A gentleman is what I call you
When I discover you to be …
A gentleman.

Pause. He is sheepish, confused by her comic acumen.

So I laugh,
'Cause I have to admit,
She absolutely got me there.
So I offer her my arm,
And when we hit the floor …

We hear an instrumental version of, At Last *by Etta James …*

Our bodies sort of …
Click together,
Hand in hand,
Toe to toe,
Somehow we seem to fit and flow

Like we've been here forever,
In some kind of crazy,
Magic dance of destiny.

And I can see from my periphery,
Every eye in the room
Has shifted from the bride and groom
Onto me and Emily.
'Cause unlike him and her,
She and me have got the chemistry of what they call,
'A handsome couple'.
So with every step,
Every dip,
Every slip
And slide
And glide
And trip,
I'm thinking,
Just you wait my dear.
I'll show you who's a gentleman.

The music fades.

The Bus Driver

Minstead Gardens,
5:05 am,
First stop on the route,
And my perfect run is already in delay when
This guy steps on but doesn't pay.
So now I have to do my 'tough guy' thing …

He assumes his 'tough guy' stance.

Step off the bus Sir,
Step off the bus,
Step off the bus
Sir, Step off the bus.

After I repeat this several dozen times,
He realises,
That he will *never* get past me.
So he steps off the bus and declares I am,
An f-ing something something.

72   Once Upon a Bridge

Then I accelerate to stay on track
And make up the time he cost me.

In the past two years I've learned,
A lot of interesting new swear words in my job:
Dopey Git,
F-ing Moron,
F-ing Muppet,
F-ing Wanker.
And my favourite of all so far …

Bloody F-ing Numb Nut.

Still,
Perfect run or not,
I hold on to my cool,
Stay sharp,
And remember what I'm driving
Is a ten tonne,
Thirty-six foot long,
Fourteen foot high,
Nine foot wide,
Fire engine red,
Double decker vehicle.
It's a big responsibility,
But to the people on the street I am invisible.
I am the bright red monster they cannot see,
And yet they duck,
They dive,
They bob,
They weave though these moving lumps of metal
As if they are not there.

A London bus is like the horse of Troy,
If you don't keep your cool,
It can unleash catastrophe.
Last week the powers that be terminated a driver's
     contract
When he failed to see a pedestrian
Who walked into his path with her head down in her
     phone.
In the investigation they said to him,
Though the pedestrian was in the wrong,

Once Upon a Bridge 73

We can see from the camera,
You are still the one who failed to be her eyes.

Each night,
When my daughters go to bed,
Before they lay their heads to rest
We close our eyes and pray,
Dearest Lord,
Help me be,
The people's eyes that don't see me.
And I think,
Someone must have heard us,
On the 5th of May.

A Woman

So as a consequence of
My grandmother's Piccadilly fall,
The story sparked in her son,
And her son in me,
Let's just say …
A lexical knowledge
Of the more unsavoury miscarriages of justice
Between our two great nations
Over the past eight hundred years.

At the age of ten,
For Halloween,
When all the girls dressed up
As Ginger, Baby, Scary, Sporty and Posh,
I dressed up as Emma Thompson from
In the Name of the Father.
For my robes I wore a pair of black bin liners,
And my wig was a chunk off an Aran jumper.
I then took to knocking on every door in Renmore
     declaiming …

She does a perfect impression of Emma Thompson in, In the Name of the Father.

Someone,
Either that man,
Or his superiors,
Ordered these people be used as scapegoats!
When their only crime was to be bloody well Irish,

74   Once Upon a Bridge

In the wrong place,
At the wrong time!

She's good at doing that. She knows it.

Ten years later,
My scholarship interview for Cambridge University went
    something like this ...

She clears her throat and impersonates the interview panel.

Can you give us a reason why you want to study English law?

I can give you ten,
I say,
The Birmingham Six and the Guildford Four.

She ever so smugly continues.

So when I graduated
And moved to London to study for the bar
With my first class honours Cambridge degree,
My Gran well ...
She had this advice for me:
London is a brute!
She said.
London is a beast!
Sooner or later it'll have you crying in a toilet,
But you dry your eyes,
Show no fear,
Crack on and don't look back,
Ye hear me now?
And if you want to get from A to B
For blazes sake don't look them in the eye.
Look down the barrel of the path in front of you.
Not at the passers by
Or I swear to Jaysus,
You'll be left for dead.
You think Oliver Cromwell sailed into County Wexford and
    said ...
'Oh, lads, do you mind,
If I take a biteen of that land there?'
No!
He slaughtered the lot of them!

> *Which is what they'll do to you,*
> *If you don't look sharp.*
>
> *And for the love of god,*
> *Don't be saying sorry*
> *When you've nothing to be sorry for.*
> *And for the love of god,*
> *Don't darken my door*
> *If you start talking like a la-di-da.*
> *It's soft Ts I want to hear,*
> *Soft as the butter in Ballymaloe.*
> *And it's …*
> *'I.*
> *Am.*
> *After.'*
> *Not …*
> *'I.*
> *Have.*
> *Recently.'*
> *If they can't understand what you say,*
> *That's on them not you!*

She takes a breath before returning to herself.

> Still when I got to Cambridge,
> A knee scraped,
> Wind blown Galway girl,
> Scooped up off a housing estate
> And flung among those gallant halls
> And ancient walls,
> And pontoon picnics on the river Cam,
> With Geoffreys and Persephones
> From castles and country manors,

She slowly and expertly slides into full-on Sloane Ranger.

> I became let's just say …
> Slightly seduced by the incantations of the upper classes.
> The sleek curve of their vowels
> And the crisp collars of their consonants
> Assumed an air of status
> I could not resist.
> And it was not long
> Before I was saying

76   Once Upon a Bridge

Are,
Instead of or.
And ho*t,*
Instead of hot,
And tha*t,*
And ha*t,*
And wai*t,*
And grea*t.*
And sometimes at nigh*t,*
When I'm ou*t* on a da*te.*
And some handsome fellow thinks I'm from Ken*t,*
I don'*t* always correc*t* him.
Because I was learning fast,
From their impressions,
Of the way I spoke,
And their casual jokes about potatoes and the famine,
That if you want to get along
This side of the pond,
It helps to play down the Paddy.
Then over the years,
It just became … easier I guess
To be English over here,
And Irish over there,
When I'm home to Gran for the Christmas visit.

That's hardly tantamount to treason …

Is it?

A Man

So I Google it,
When I get home.
Rules of Being a Gentleman.

He lists them on his fingers.

Be on time,
Open doors,
Buy an umbrella,
Own a pen,
Ring your mum,
Don't say '*slut*'.
Never refer to things as '*gay*'.
On the second date offer to pay,

Once Upon a Bridge   77

But if she insists,
Let her split the bill.
Because ...

Delighted he knows the lingo.

'The Future Is Female.'

So I splash out on this fancy pen,
And send a monogrammed card to her office.
One line:
Thank you for the dance.
On our first date,
I tell her I work in renewable energy,
Which is ... partially true.
I wait for the second date to explain that exactly what I do
Is research analytics for an investment bank
In the heart of the Square Mile,
Appraising publicly listed green energy companies,
Advising traders to buy or sell
Based on my appraisal of their market price.
I leave a pause.

He leaves a pause.

Let her chew.
Swallow.
Then I land the plane.

He goes in for the passionate 'big sell'.

Look, I know what people think of City Boys,
That they're a bunch of corrupt,
Money hungry,
Maniacal pricks
But I need you to know
I do what I do
Because we live in a capitalist system,
Which means if green energy is not profitable,
It will fail.
And if it fails,
And we continue to plunder the earth,
In the way we've been
Since the Industrial Revolution,
The ice caps will melt,

78   Once Upon a Bridge

The penguins will die,
Cities will drown,
Fires will burn,
And if that means I have to spend twenty-five grand a year
Wining and dining dickhead hedge fund managers
In Michelin star restaurants,
Pouring champagne down their gullets
Stuffing coke up their noses,
So they invest in wind farms in the Hebrides,
Then that is what I'll do to ensure a future
For my children and my children's children.

Twelve months later,
She's moved to London,
And we're married,
With a baby on the way.

Boom! He is delighted with himself.

Then we start looking for a house,
Which is tricky,
Because *she's* not fussed,
But *I* want Hampstead Heath.
Red brick,
Park view,
Rooftop terrace:
I want to look out my window and see Ricky Gervais out
    walking his dog,
And after *six* years of ducking and diving in the City
I am *that* close.

He gestures a centimetre with his index finger and thumb.

I just need a little time,
Keep my Emily sweet,
So while she's off looking at some shit box in zone nine,
I do a cheeky deal on this place off the Fulham Road.
Five minutes from the River Thames.
Half an hour to work.
Couldn't be more perfect.

He is chuffed with himself.

You wanna see her face.
You wanna *see*.

Her.
Face.
It.
Was.
Priceless.
And she's all,
I can't believe you went and bought this.

He confides quietly to the audience.

I didn't.
It's rented.
Four grand a month,
But I keep that between my teeth –
'Cause there's a promotion coming up at work
And the money I'll be on?
In another year?
We'll be strolling on the Heath.
So there's no point in stressing her out is there?

He touches his stomach to gesture the baby. Deep down he knows he has railroaded her.

And if I may offer in my defense,
A *gentleman*
Spares no expense.

The Bus Driver

Route 430 has thirty-five stops,
From Knightsbridge to Minstead Gardens.
I'm halfway through,
Doing well,
When the first wave of rush hour hits:
Hard hats,
Name tags,
Polyester uniforms.
Then the second wave of suits arrive,
In a cloud of perfume and colognes
And shoes not designed to stand in.
They all slot into their seats,
Disappear into their phones,
And I roll without a hitch.
My perfect run is going like a dream.

80   Once Upon a Bridge

At 6:18 am I cross the Thames
And turn left
Up Fulham Palace Road,
With precision timing:
Cromwell Mews,
Cromwell Place,
Cromwell Road,
Then past Cromwell Gardens.
Four streets?
Whoa,
This Cromwell was some clever son.
Then five,
Four,
Three,
Two,
One,
I glide to a stop
At the Victoria and Albert Museum,
Where I take my coffee break,
And think back to the day I did my final drivers' test.
Man, I was so nervous.
As I wait for the examiner to tell me the result,
I had to hide my fingers
In case she sees them shake and marks me down.
You got kids?
She says,
Yes I do, I say.
Congratulations.
Their dad is now the driver of a London bus.
Good luck and don't forget,
Your cargo is precious,
So take great pride in the service you deliver.

A beat.

Then I check the time,
And three,
Two,
One,
I turn the engine on,
And head back towards the river.

Once Upon a Bridge 81

A Man
Okay … before I go into this next bit,
I need to preface it.

Sometime in late April 2017,
There's a meeting on the office floor,
On account of an official complaint,
About –
Wait for it –
Micro aggressive behaviour
In the financial services industry.

Micro.
Aggressive.
Behaviour.
Micro.
In the financial services industry.

Mock fear.

Oh deary me,
Who'd've thought it?

Still this particular complaint
Went all the way to the attention of the CEO,
Who in light of shifting social attitudes,
*Would like to run a series of workshops all employees must
   undergo.*
Next thing,
Some hairy legged hippy is pulling out a pie chart
   going …

He does a mocking impression.

*The ratio of men to women in the banking sector
Is around 5:1 for analysts and associates
And 17:1 for an MD
Now what does that tell us about gender imbalance financial
   playing field?*

Fuck.
Me.
I spend the rest of the morning doing role plays,
*About the adverse effects of micro aggressions,
And the systemic implications of complimenting hair.*

82   Once Upon a Bridge

At tea break word gets out about
Who cracked this total Guinness fart of an idea.
I look across at Linda,
Sipping on her decaf chai latte,
As if butter wouldn't melt.

Of course.

There was once a time,
Linda and me,
We …
Well …
Let's just say we were quite the pair,

He's about to tell one story, then decides to tell another.

Down the Blackfriars,
Four nights a week,
Propping up the bar,
Closing massive deals,
Drinking billionaire investors under the table.
I'd keep the champagne flowing,
And whatever else was going,
While she worked her magic charm.
We were just unstoppable.
Then one night,
We were down at Tramp
Pressing flesh with this Middle Eastern oil guy prick,
And it's going well.
We're up on the dance floor,
And she's like
You go get the drinks in,
I'll keep him here,
I love this song.
So I toddle off to order shots
But when I come back,
They're gone.
And me,
Left standing at the side line,
Tray of shots in hand,
Trying to spot her dress
In a sea of swaying bodies.
But she's long away by this time,

In a taxi cab
Headed back to his hotel room
To press more flesh I guess.

So yeah.
He pisses off,
Quelle surprise?
She discovers she's 'with child',
And decides to *have* the baby on her own.

Now she's fighting to stay in the game,
Without the coke and bubbles
While I'm still out there *killing* it,
And *she's* home watching Dora the Explorer on her iPad
    for her troubles.

Well what did she expect?
That everything would stop for *her*?
Is it *my* fault it didn't?
No.
Bitter *is* she?
Yes.
'Cause she sees me with my salary,
And my gorgeous pregnant American international
    lawyer wife
And it's *killing* her
'Cause she *knows* she could be Emily.
But *she* messed up,
She blew her chance to have the picture perfect life.
So she goes and files this 'micro aggression' nonsense
So when the next promotion comes along,
She'll squeeze in,
Ladies first,
To get ahead of me
Even though numbers wise,
I'm *way* past her.
Linda, Linda, Linda,
If that's the game you want to play,
I'll show you who's the master.

The Bus Driver
I'm approaching Fulham now,
The final stretch,

84   Once Upon a Bridge

And I allow myself
To picture the look of shock on my boss's face
As he watches me,
The golden boy,
Bring home the *perfect* run.
And I think,
Tonight, that's it!
I don't care what it costs.
We are ordering a takeaway,
Because I swear to god –

A Woman
I did it!
After seven years of study,
Twenty-five thousand pounds in debt,
And one failed relationship due to appalling work/life
    balance,
Which was both my fault *and* worth it,
I bag myself an interview
With Kingston Manly Chambers,
The top ranked criminal law firm this side of the Equator.
The golden goose.
The golden fleece.
The golden egg,
You get the picture.
It's a big deal,
A very,
Very,
Very big deal.
This is fecking it I swear.

So it's Friday morning,
5th of May –

A Man
Or as I call it,
Promotion day.

The Bus Driver
I slide through the North End Road,
How do you like *them* apples sir?
How do they look to you?

The Man
I can almost smell the dew of Hampstead Heath
Drifting through the window.
My alarm goes off,
And I am out of bed
And up to check the markets.

The Bus Driver
And I'm thinking,
Will we get Japanese or Indian?
Or will we let the kids decide?

A Woman
I do pilates,
Hit the shower,
Then make up –

The Bus Driver
Then onto Mulgrave Road,
Like I'm driving to a fanfare –

A Man
For the past two weeks I've been slugging it out
With Ms Chai Latte,
For this chief analyst position.
She's been making ground,
But I think sharp,
And get an inside tip on 'Zephyr Enterprises'.
A green energy group that's about to go south.
So I pull a cheeky move,
And leak the news to some big investors
Before it all goes public –

He's defensive.

Insider trading,
Is illegal,
Yes,
A crime,
I know,
But they're all at it.
It's fine,
Just don't get caught.
Besides my boss Billy Boy,

86   Once Upon a Bridge

He's not fussed
And it pays off like a dream for me,
Leaving Linda in the dust.
What I wouldn't give to see her face
When she wakes up to that this morning –

The Bus Driver
Fulham Pools.
Fulham Cross.
Clear as day.
I can't believe it's happening.
I check the time –

A Woman
I check the news,
Press my suit,
Do my hair,
Grab my phone,
And one quick spray of Jo Malone –

The Bus Driver
Then onto Lillie Road,
Which is absolutely clear.

A Man
So I do a hundred crunches
And get on my running gear –

The Bus Driver
Then onto Kingswood Road.

A Woman
Then stand before the mirror,
To drill my opening line:

She does a very posh English accent.

Hello, nice to meet you.
Hello, nice to meet you.

A Man
And stretch,
Stretch,
Stretch,
Stretch.

Once Upon a Bridge   87

The Bus Driver
Bothwell Street.
Clear as day.
Amazing.

A Woman
You're amazing,
You're amazing,
You're amazing to your core.

A Man
Then I pick a running route –

The Bus Driver
Bishop's Park.

A Woman
Check I've got the right address,
Put it in my GPS,
And it's up and out the door thinking,
How proud of me
My Gran would be,
If she could see me now –

The Bus Driver
Just keep the pace.
Just keep the pace.
Slow and steady wins the race.

A Man
The streets are nice and empty,
Just the way I like them.
My 'interview' with Bill
Is scheduled at 9:15 am –
I'm the favourite by a long stretch,
But there's two more players in the race:

He lists the contenders …

Some bloke from overseas no one's ever even heard of,
Then Linda bringing up the rear,
Too slow to keep the pace.

The Bus Driver
And I swear in all my life,
Never has a London bus ever been more punctual.

88   Once Upon a Bridge

A Man

Time to bang out a quick five k –
To get the system pumping.

The Bus Driver

Then I'm onto Fulham Palace Road,
A bunch of school kids drag their feet towards the stop
But I keep going,
Knowing they'll be late for school,
But if I wait
I won't be on course to hit the depot exactly to the second,
So I'm doing under twenty when I hit the Thames.

A Woman

Heading up across the bridge now,
That leads to Putney station,
My parents' wedding song blasting in my ears,
Gerry and the Pacemakers.
I always play this when I need to puff my feathers.

A Man

Back it up,
Back it up,
Back it up,
Back it up!
You've got to *know* what happened.
Just *before* the bridge,
I get a call from work.
*There's a childcare cover issue with a candidate for this morning's
    interviews.*
They're flipping you to nine.

Sure that's fine,
No problem.

What?
I was bang on time.
Now I'm late.
How the fuck that come about,
When they've only got three candidates …?

Childcare cover.
It doesn't take a genius to work out who's the mother.

Once Upon a Bridge   89

The Bus Driver
So I'm gliding over Putney Bridge –

A Man
Running –

A Woman
Walking –

A Man
Running –

The Bus Driver
Across the shimmering river –

A Woman
My two eyes fixed
Dead ahead,
Just like my grandma said.
Flat shoes.
No heels.
To hell with that.
If I want to walk on stilts,
I'll join the bloody circus.
Shoulder bag.
Right side.
The corners of my brand new,
Jet black,
Massimo Dutti coat buffeting the breeze
And mise,
Gráinne Mhaol,
The Pirate Queen,
Tacking across the grey vein of the River Thames,
To claim my treasure.
Then I see this jogger to my right,
Face all pink and white and creased with effort,
Heading right towards me in the shadow of the sun,
I'm thinking …
Running for the train or training for the run?

A Man
That fucking
Latte sucking bitch –

90   Once Upon a Bridge

She stitched me up
I swear.

The Bus Driver
And I'm thinking,
In just six minutes,
I'll be driving –

A Woman
Walking –

A Man
Running –

The Bus Driver
Through those depot doors
Like a lion to his lair –

A Man
Hell no.
She's not pulling that on me,
Not today,
No way.
Now I'm proper pissed,
The red mist rising in me
So I'm running –

A Woman
Walking –

A Man
Running –

The Bus Driver
The cheers and waves and whistles,
Of my friends and colleagues calling
There he goes,
The man who showed the powers that be,
The man who single handedly,
Restored dignity to the people of the morning shift.

A Man
Now I'm powering over Putney Bridge,
Trying to make up the time,
Racing in the inside,
Where the shadow meets the sun,

And I see this woman dead ahead,
With one foot stuck in *my* side,
Where I intend to run,
And I'm thinking,
Uh oh,
Here we go,
Here's another one.
Christ they're everywhere.
Getting closer now,
And I'm –

The Bus Driver
Driving –

A Woman
Walking –

A Man
Running –
Get out of my lane!
Non-verbal micro aggression?
You want to take me on?
Well come on!
Come and have a go as well,
You just keep strolling on,
I'll toss you out the window,
'Cause I'll tell you straight my dear,
If it's one thing this world does not need,
It's another.
Fucking.
LINDA!!!

The Bus Driver
He was like a rugby man,
He hit her like a rugby man
Straight into her shoulder.

And with the blow,
She creases like an old tin can …
Ankle,
Knee,
Shin …

92 Once Upon a Bridge

A Woman
And I collapse under the force of him
As his body hits my body ...

The Bus Driver
And her balance goes,
Her right foot flips,
And tangles in his legs,
And he pushes her away.

A Woman
And I am falling,
Sinking ...

The Bus Driver
Down towards the concrete.
With no hands out to break her fall,
And smack.

A Woman
And the world tips upside down ...

The Bus Driver
The momentum of the crash
Dragging her beyond the kerb –
Into the black abyss of Putney Bridge,
Towards the front tyre of my bus.

A Woman
Then a roar,
As if some bloodied monster
Ran right past my head –

The Bus Driver
I grab the wheel,
Bite down with my fingers,
Knuckles popping white,
As I swerve sharp to avoid her
Sending screams and roars
Up through the bus
And all the time I pray
And pray,
I don't feel her
Tangle in the back wheels of the bus.
Then stop.

Breathe.
In.
Out.
In.
Out.
In.
Then swallow down my swollen heart into my swollen chest,
And watch in disbelief as this man runs away
Across the river.
Small.
Smaller.
Smaller.
Gone.
I push the exit button,
Step off …

And there she is
Lying on the pavement forty feet away.
Still as still can be.
Her face,
Ship sail white.
The wings of her black coat
Flapping,
Flailing,
Failing to lift her off the ground.
And she looks …
She looks as if a sparrow fell from the clouds,
Startled,
Wondering why she's not still in the sky.
Then finally she moves.
I breathe a sigh,
And see her tears,
Like the river below us rolling free.
And as I get close I hear her cry …

A Woman
> *Why me?*
> *Why me?*
> *Why me?*

The Bus Driver
> It's a very good question.
> And in that moment,

94   Once Upon a Bridge

I have no answer for her.
I ask if she is badly hurt,
But her lips cannot command themselves to fashion
    a reply.
Instead, her eyes scanning the cement,
As if in search of her lost dignity
To soften the shock of the fall.
I wait,
My supervisor's satellite all the while,
Watching from above.
Through the windows of my bus,
The passengers look on,
Some out of concern,
Some from irritation
And I think where are your manners?
Still, the city drums its fingernails against my better
    judgement
To remain and help this woman.
So I give her a note with my information,
So she can recommence her day.
Then I step back onto my bus,
The precious seconds of my perfect run,
Now slowly bled away.

A Man

And when I get home,
Emily is calling me,
The office rang,
You're late –
I know –
I'll drive you in –
We're all a fuss,
The pair of us,
Trying to get out the door,
And as she does my tie
She kisses me,
What's that?
She says
What's what?
Say I –

> *You either stole my perfume*
> *Or you're having an affair.*
> But I know what she means,
> I can just about smell it,
> Lingering in the air.

So innocent ... relieved even ...

> *Oh! Oh!*
> *I was running over Putney Bridge*
> *When this woman hit me*
> *Coming the other way.*

She buys it.

> I place my lips on her
> To kiss away her worries.
> *Now come on love I'm late.*

A Woman

> So there I am,
> Clothes lined to the ground,
> Power dressed and freak showed,
> The smell of him still on me,
> As strangers gather round to help,
> Yet still careful not to get caught up ...

> *Are you hurt love?*
> *Are you hurt?*
> *Are you hurt love?*
> *Are you hurt?*

> But I'm too numb
> Too anesthetised by shock to answer,
> Too distracted by the shards of glass
> Twinkling in the gutter.

She shakes herself out of it.

> Oh god!
> My phone!
> My phone's destroyed –
> *What time is it?*
> *Eight o'clock?*
> My golden fleece.
> My interview.

96   Once Upon a Bridge

Addled ...

> I have to be at Farringdon by nine,
> Fifty-two minutes away ...
> *What time did you say ....?*
> I've got to reach my destination.
> I try to rise.
> *Ow!*
> Someone takes my arm –
> *Don't touch me please! Don't touch me!*
> Then I grab my phone, my bag, my pride,
> And jelly kneed,
> They watch me stumble towards the station.

He's crushed ...

The Bus Driver
> I arrive back at the depot,
> Seventeen minutes late,
> Knock on my boss's door,
> To explain my reason,
> And that I need to report an incident
> On Putney Bridge.
> He makes a note,
> And says he will review it.
> I'm nervous now because of that other guy they dismissed.
> *Be the eyes that don't see me ...*
> Maybe they will watch the film
> And see something I didn't see,
> Something that I didn't do,
> Or failed to have done better.
> *Twenty-five thousand pounds* a year ...
> *Twelve times* the salary for the same job I did back home.
> I cannot fail now,
> I cannot afford to lose this opportunity
> After taking my family so far,
> But with the satellite technology they'll soon tell *me*
>   what happened,
> If I did or did not respond
> In the way that they expect ...

Once Upon a Bridge   97

If I am the piece of rotten fruit
They inspect and then
Reject.

A Woman
I arrive at Farringdon,
With two-and-a-half minutes to spare,
Try to run to the toilet to
Wipe my face and brush my hair,
But I'm called in to a room
Where three Senior Councils wait for me:
Two men,
One woman,
Wearing what I can only describe as …
Fifty shades of tweed.
They look like the contestants on *Countdown*.
Not the class of Casual Friday I was hoping for.
I thought it'd be more like *The Good Wife* …
The head panelist shuts the door
And thrusts out an open palm for me to shake.

She smothers the pain.

Hello, nice to meet you.

A shock of pain shoots up my arm
From where the heel of my hand
Came in contact with the pavement.
Gingerly, I offer up my swollen paw
For the other two to rattle.

She does an English accent.

Hello.
Hia –
How are you? –
Sorry, I mean, sorry …
Nice to meet you.
Sorry …

We sit at a ridiculously large mahogany table,
Intended no doubt,
To remind one where one lies on the food chain.
So I casually remark …

98   Once Upon a Bridge

She tries too hard to impress in an English accent.

> *How reminiscent it is of*
> *The table they use to swear new barristers in at Middle Temple,*
> *Being made of wood from The Golden Goose – I mean Golden Hind,*
> *The ship Sir Francis Drake,*
> *Sailed round the world in.*

Her banter goes down like a lead balloon.

> Tough crowd.
> My banter falls on solid stone.

> As they shuffle their papers,
> I see my coat on the adjacent chair
> Has gray streaks of dirt running up its back
> From the waist to the hem,
> And on its cuff,
> The rectangle of a cigarette butt dangles by a strand
>   of hair.
> Shrapnel from this morning's battle on the bridge
> And as I sit
> Hypnotized by it,
> I realise they're asking me a question.

She impersonates the interviewer.

> *The role of a criminal advocate in our organisation*
> *Is to handle a myriad of serious violent crime:*
> *Murder,*
> *Kidnapping,*
> *Sexual assault,*
> *Spousal abuse*
> *And human trafficking will be the staple of your working day.*
> *In light of this,*
> *How important is it to you –*
> *With regard to how valuable our time is here –*
> *To entertain the more inconsequential cases,*
> *Such as petty theft,*
> *Or minor assault,*
> *Especially when there is little chance of a successful outcome?*

A beat.

Once Upon a Bridge 99

I try to focus on the words,
But he rambles on so long,
By the time he's reached the end,
I've forgotten the beginning.
Petty theft ...
Minor assault ...
What I'm picking up from what he's throwing down is,
We don't want to hire someone
Who's going to waste our time
With cases that won't make the news.
Meanwhile,
Screeching violins of pain arrive,
Shooting up my back,
From this morning's misdemeanour –

Sorry, just a minute.

I take a sip of water,
Try to stall for time,
But from underneath my bra strap,
The tweezer pinch of a damaged nerve
From where my assailant's body collided into mine.
Begins to whine for my attention,
Another sip.
My hand wobbles to the glass.
There's nothing I can do to mask my trembling fingers.

Is everything all right?
They ask.

She falters into an Irish accent.

Sorry – I mean pardon me, it's just ...
I just ...
This morning before I got here ...
I'm just after having ...
I mean I'm only just ...
On my way over ...
Sorry it's just that I'm only just after having a fall ...
The words tumble out my mouth
Like bits of broken leprechaun,
As my inner state betrays my outer self.
They confer amongst each other as to what the fecking
    hell it is I'm saying.

100   Once Upon a Bridge

She impersonates them murmuring.

>*What was that?*
>*What's she after?*

Loud, as if she speaks a different language.

>*Pardon us,*
>*We can't quite make out*
>*What is it you said ...*

>*I said that I am after –*
>*Yes, yes, yes,*
>*But what is it you need,*
>*Exactly what is it you're after?*

Then that's it.
Something snaps in me
Like the trunk of a tree
On the leg of an eight-hundred-year-old bucking raging
    monster.
And I dunno if it's lunacy of them not understanding
The tongue of their own nation,
Or the memory of my tumble on the bridge,
Coupled with my granny's fall in Piccadilly station
Now banging like a pound of flesh,
Off the chambers of my heart but I say –

She blows.

>*No!*
>*I'm AFTER having a fall.*
>*FALL as in fallen down.*
>*I.*
>*Am.*
>*After.*
>*As in ...*
>*I.*
>*Have.*
>*Just.*
>*Recently.*
>*Had*
>*A*
>*Fall,*
>*When I was shoved by a jogger*

On Putney Bridge
In what you might call 'A minor assault'.
And what I might call, 'Attempted murder',
Because the fact is,
His deliberate action in the recent hour almost caused my death.
And if that falls below your 'golden standard' of what class of
   crime,
Is worthy of your attention,
Then this interview has been a colossal waste of
My 'Valuable' time!

I sink the glass of water,
And hammer it down on their bullshit fecking table.
Then bag.
Coat.
Up and out.
Cigarette butt flying through the air,
As the canon of the slamming door
Blasts up through the building.
Then I head to the nearest police station,
Where I report how at approximately 7:40 this morning,
While crossing Putney Bridge,
A white male in this thirties
Assaulted me with clear intent to injure, maim or kill.

As my grandma used to always say
If you go down,
Go down in flames.

They won't forget you still.

The Bus Driver
I head up to the staff room,
Which is now in full voice
With the changing of the guard,
As daytime radio goes to war with the slap of dominos.
I say hi to Barry White.
Barry's surname isn't White,
They just call him that because he's the only white guy on
   this shift.
He doesn't mind,
I'm told.

102   Once Upon a Bridge

The tongues of up to forty nations
Can pass through this station in any one day.
I sit and watch my fellow drivers.
Some of them have climbed mountains to be here.
Literally.
And where did they decide to go?
Great Britain.
They came to the country that conquered the world,
So that they can conquer their past,
And seek a better future for their children,
And their children's children.
I get a text from my eldest daughter,
Can we order pizza tonight?
I send her back an emoji frown,
And tell her to stop running down the credit her mother's
    phone.
I collect my things,
And when I get home,
My wife's tired feet are up on the coffee table.
Our kids are in the yard,
Pretending they're on *Strictly,*
And through the open window,
The breeze blows in the smell of barbecues,
And the tunes float in from the corner pub,
Where the DJ spins the records.

The music pops on: Roland Alphonso's cover of Whiter Shade
of Pale.

He dances. He's very good.

And to my wife I say,
Come dance with me?
And she say's
No, no, no, no, no.
Come dance with me?
And she say's
No, no, no, no, no.
But when she sees me move I know she can't resist.
And so we dance around our living room,
Like it's our wedding day.
One – two – three,
One – two – three,

Once Upon a Bridge   103

One – two – three.
And I'm thinking as we spin and sway,
Between the table and the chairs …

He slows his movement as the reality of what happened that morning lands on him.

How I would not be dancing now,
If I hit that girl today.

Life is a dance, is it not?
And it goes past
Faster than the beat of a metronome,
And so we must dance to every song,
We must dance to every beat
From start to finish and finish to start.
For shadows we are,
And like shadows we depart.

The music fades.

A Woman
First,
They put police out in the area:
Fulham High Street,
Along the river. Looking for a match,
White male,
Thirties,
Average build,
Brown eyes,
Short brown hair.
That narrows it down to what?
Several hundred thousand suspects.
Of course he could have been here on a business trip,
And possibly left town,
Which the lead detective is at pains to remind me is
Like looking in a haystack for a needle that's not there.
She calls me once a week to say,
Please be assured,
We're doing absolutely everything we can
Given our increasingly limited resources:
A word salad of a party line
Designed to lower my expectations.

104 Once Upon a Bridge

In the meantime,
I do my best not let the moment on the bridge
Hold my future by its ankles.
So I drift through fruitless interviews,
But all my hunger for the law is
Now siphoned into a ravenous rage to see him crushed
  into the ground
Just as he crushed me.
Still, I pick up work at a legal firm,
Covering maternity leave,

And on my way home each day
My eye is pulled to the passengers of taxi cars,
And smokers outside clubs and bars
For his likeness in the men.
Even though deep down I know,
I wouldn't recognise him if I saw him again.
And in bed at night as sleep fails to arrive,
The 'what ifs' start rolling in like waves,
And I can't help but think,
If it was Claddagh Bridge in Galway,
Not Putney Bridge in London,
It wouldn't have happened at all,
And if it did,
He'd at least have been a different kind of man.
He'd've stalled and said,
Oh my god I'm so sorry love,
Are you okay?
Ah it's yourself,
Sure didn't I know your gran.
You're the spit of her in every way.

But I know
From when I was a child,
Looking at her ballroom nose
That London isn't like that,
There are no scales of justice here,
To balance out every tiny microcosmic wrong.
And that's why I'm still on that bridge,
While he simply just …
Ran on.

Once Upon a Bridge   105

The Bus Driver
  Okay,
  Let me think,
  When was it …?
  I'm thinking it w –

A Man
  August.
  It was August.
  I get the promotion by the way.
  Quelle surprise?
  Life is sweet.
  Emily's on leave
  Awaiting the birth of our first baby
  Who is kicking like a Barcelona striker,
  I get my first six figure bonus –
  Score.
  Fulham's soon to be no more,
  Which means, you guessed it –
  Hampstead Heath.
  And on the 17th at 6 pm,
  I'm bidding on a house *two streets* from Jamie Oliver.
  I cannot *wait* to see her face …

As **A Man** *revels in this moment,* **The Bus Driver** *patiently recommences.*

The Bus Driver
  So I think it was mid August maybe?

A Man
  I'm on the Tube to work that morning,
  And the passenger opposite's reading a paper
  Massive picture splashed across the front,
  So I lean in to read the headline underneath …

He reads to himself …

The Bus Driver
  They've been looking for this jogger for several months
    now
  But still no one was charged,
  And now the police would like to start a media campaign –

A Man
  Woman's Life Saved by London Bus Driver …

The Bus Driver

And can they use my name.
To be honest,
I wasn't sure if I wanted the attention.

A Man

After being pushed into the path of his vehicle on Putney Bridge
By a passing jogger on the 5th of May …

The cogs turn … slowly.

Putney Bridge …
Fifth of May …
Was I there that day …?

The Bus Driver

I'm quite a private person actually.
I don't like any fuss.

A Man

So I glance up at the image,
See if I might know him …

His face drops like a hot pie.

No …
That's not me.
It couldn't be …
And yet …

The Bus Driver

Still I felt obliged to help.

A Man

I get off the Tube at Piccadilly Circus.
Fall up the steps
Breathe in the morning air,
Thinking someone's playing a trick on me,
It's a joke,
A scam,
This isn't fair.
Then wham!
There I am –
I mean there it is again,
Splashed across the morning news:
Guardian,

Times,
Telegraph,
Same shirt,
Same shorts,
Same shoes as me.
In black and white and grey.
Putney Bridge Psychotic Monster,

Police Seek Help To Identify Suspect ... Captured on Video?

He falls into abject despair.

Oh no ...
You have got to be bloody kidding me!

The Bus Driver
And so my supervisor calls me in to show me
The footage of the incident,
Taken from the bus ahead.

The audience sees the actual footage of the incident on Putney Bridge on a large screen. It plays twice. The first time without him speaking. The second time, he speaks as each moment plays out in slow motion.

The Bus Driver
And for the first time since that day
I see each second frame by frame.
I see her walk.

A Man
No ...

The Bus Driver
I see him hit.

A Man
Wait ...

The Bus Driver
I see her fall.

A Man
She ...

The Bus Driver
I see me swerve.

108　Once Upon a Bridge

A Man
But she …

The Bus Driver
I see him run away.

A Man
This is *non*sense.

The Bus Driver
And it's only at that moment
I realize that I was that *close* from her.

He shows a centimetre with his thumb and index finger.

And I think that *she* probably did not realize,
How *close* she was from *me*,
And *he* does not realise
Because when she hits the ground
He does not stop to see.

A Man
She hit *ME!*

The Bus Driver
Instead he runs.

A Man
She could see me.

The Bus Driver
And runs –

The Man
Clear as day.

The Bus Driver
And runs.
Then disappears,
Into the foliage of eight point nine million people.

A Man
She wouldn't get out of the way!

The Bus Driver
But even still,
He must have heard her cry,

Once Upon a Bridge   109

And that is why
To this day I swear it was on purpose.

A Man

I try to breathe,
Heave but nothing comes,
Nothing but the memory of that morning
Coming up in chunks.

Addled ... self aware.

Shit!

The Bus Driver

I'll tell you one thing.

A Man

It wasn't like that.
They've got it wrong!
I'm not getting done for this.

The Bus Driver

And it's as simple as this:
He nearly made me kill that woman.
And when he did,
He did not think of me,
Or my wife,
Or my children,
Who now don't recognise their dad –
Who tucked them in the night before ...
Walked out the door to work
And returned a different person.

The Bus Driver

No, he did not think of me,
Or if I lost my job and could no longer support my family.
Because to this *snake*
I'm just another no one driver
Of another *invisible* bus
He cares not if he crushes,
Because he will always wriggle free.

A cool resolve comes over him.

So I look at the police and say,
What can I do to catch this guy?

And that is why my daughters get
The day off school to watch their father on TV.
And as the camera rolls on the *Good Morning Britain*
    breakfast show
With a million pairs of eyes on me,
I smile into the lens and think
Just you wait my friend.
Your horse of Troy is on its way.
I'll show you who's a nobody.

A Man
I get text from Billy Boy –
Come see me straight away.
So I cab it over to Cheapside in three minutes flat,
Punch the lift and hit my office floor.
Fifty traders at their desks,
All glued to their computers.

He's relieved.

No one blinks an eye.
Too busy making proper coin to care
About what's happening in the news.

Billy's in his office.
Back faced to the door.
Newspaper tossed beside him on the floor,
Yours truly on the cover.
So I go,
All right mate,
I know,
I know,
It's all a massive mix up
But there's a very simple explanation –

But as he turns,
My mate Billy Boy displays a face
That does not care to listen.
It's been brought to my attention,
That earlier this year,
You leaked private data
About a listed company
Two days before the share price dropped,
Resulting in our bank avoiding a loss of several million Euro.

Once Upon a Bridge   111

Yeah but Billy they're all at it –
Come on –
You know how these things go ...

Apparently he doesn't today ...

He passes me a document:
My resignation letter,
Conveniently back dated,
To August 10,
And he says,
Which would you prefer,
Police or pen?

So I choose my only option.

An odd memory pops up ...

Rule number four of being a gentleman.
When I get home Emily's in the kitchen,
Laptop on the table.
Every time the footage ends,
She slaps it back,
To play it again.

My mom got you those sneakers.
She said now that he's married my daughter,
What do you get for the man who has everything?
I said get him running shoes.

I open my mouth to offer a defence –
She slams the space bar once again,
Freezing the frame at the deed,
And you can just make out my face.

It was May,
You were late,
The perfume lady ...

And the prosecution rests its case.

We even look alike,
She says,
The hair,
The shoulder shape,
The stance,

112   Once Upon a Bridge

Say,
If you met her at a wedding,
You could've asked her for a dance.

He withers ...

Her hand slips down to her stomach.
I'm having a girl by the way.

I.
Not *we.*
A single pronoun sentences me,
To a life,
Without a wife and daughter.

He becomes desperate.

She grabs her bag,
Moves to leave –
No,
No,
No,
And with a day of whiskey sweating through each pore,
I block her path towards the door.

A tearful, crumbing, pathetic command.

Emily!
You're not leaving me,
I will never let it happen,
I will never let you go,
I will not allow it!
No, no, no, no,
No!

But Emily,
She keeps her cool.
Takes her stand,
Meets my gaze,
And with her suitcase in her hand she says,

What you gonna do?
Push me too?

Once Upon a Bridge   113

A Woman

Here's a little joke I wrote.
What does non-renewable energy
And public sympathy have in common?
Eventually,
They will both run out.

She gestures a joyless drumroll.

Bah-dum … doof …

By October of that year,
They still haven't caught him,
Or have a clue of who he might be,
This trainer wearing,
Latter day Lord Lucan.
The investigation stalls,
The people's thirst for justice wanes.
The police had wanted me to come forward,
Do a big splash,
Give up my anonymity,
To stoke the fire again
And smoke this fellow out of whatever hole he's hiding in.
Or whatever doe-eyed trophy wife he's hiding under.
But once you take that step …
Your name is public property,
Scrawled on the walls of the internet
Subject to whatever destiny they like for it.

Is that what I want?

I click on an article,
Putney Pusher Still At Large,
Then scroll down the comments section:
Better luck next time mate.
Look at her – Bitch deserved it.
Then down the end,
In all full caps,
Stupid cow.
I wouldn't even rape her.

I take a walk on Hampstead Heath
To clear my head and think,
If I could just phone the grave and talk to Gran,

114   Once Upon a Bridge

What would she say to me?
She'd say,
Dry your eyes,
Show fear the door,
Crack on and don't look back.
And don't unpack a second more,
Because that fucking eejit is not
Who or what you came to London for.

Thank you, Gran.
Is breá liom tú.

So I call the police,
Declining their request to use my name,
As it could hardly do much good any more,
Now the investigation's peaked.
Then I thank them for their time,
And warn them I will sue if my name is ever leaked.

The Bus Driver
One thing I know and it's as simple as this,
Someone out there knows who that guy is.
And even though the image is difficult to make out,
If he was my brother I'd know it was him.
If he was my son I'd know it was him.
If I was his sister,
Wife,
Girlfriend,
Boyfriend,
Uncle,
The barman in his local pub,
If I was his long lost cousin
Whom I'd not seen since I was a boy,
I would take one look at that pixelated face
And know that it was him.
The style of hair,
The shape and build,
The colour of the skin,
His boss would have opened up the paper that morning
    and seen his employee,
And make a decision to say nothing
Because this guy makes him money.
His cleaner must have opened up a wardrobe

Once Upon a Bridge   115

Seen those running shoes,
And make a decision to say nothing,
Because this guy pays her money.
Money.
Without question,
That's the key.
Money keeps you out of jail,
But it won't set your conscience free.

The Woman

You want to hear something else absolutely hilarious?

Some time in October
I got an email from Fifty Shades of Tweed
To say …

Regarding your interview on the fifth of May,
Your impassioned response to our opening question
Has since given us pause to reflect,
On how we prioritised our casework.
In light of this,
A position has opened up …
Blah, blah, blah …

I didn't take it.
Didn't have to.
I got kept on at that legal firm,
Apparently that woman on maternity leave went back to
    the States,
Fecked off on her husband –
Poor guy.
So I was hired,
And that was it.

Except for one last thing –

The Bus Driver

They gave me an award.
I was seventeen minutes late that day,
Seventeen minutes off the schedule,
A woman nearly died under my wheels,
And they gave me an award.
All because of some little thing my supervisor said
And boom!

116 Once Upon a Bridge

Here's a prize for being a hero.
Crazy …
Do pilots get a prize
When they fly their planes and no one dies?
No.
So if I am a hero,
Then every bus driver is a hero as far as I can see.

People always tell me,
They're so surprised that
I don't know who she is,
That I don't even know her name,
Or she never came to thank me.
The truth is,
Even though I won't forget her,
It would be difficult for me to recognise her today.

One time I saw this TV show:
Animal Rescue.
A man by a lake
Was helping a swan tangled up in fishing wire,
And when finally he sets her free,
She runs straight back to the water.
She doesn't thank him.
And that's all.
He walks away unharmed.
Tomorrow he couldn't say which swan he saved.
So you see,
I am the man who walked away,
Back into his life,
Just as it was before.
That's the prize for me.
And who is she?
The lady on the bridge is the swan on the lake.

The Bus Driver *looks at* **A Woman** *without her knowing.*

And swans do what's in their nature.

He exits.

A Woman
Fast forward to November.
Six am.

Once Upon a Bridge 117

Pitch black out.
I wake to find the streets powdered white with snow.
On the road where I live,
There's a stretch of path that's uneven and cracked,
From the roots of the trees.
I make my way to the station,
Careful not to slip,
When I see this guy striding towards me,
Not super speedy,
More just like a swift commuter pace.
So we meet at the bit
Where the concrete's all split,
And we stop,
And he says,
Careful there, it's wonky.
And I go,
Yeah, I know,
And smile 'cause …
Wonky …
So I sway to my right to let him pass.
But he sways to his left to do the same,
So then I sway left to let *him* go,
But *he* sways right for *me*,
So now we're both smiling,
Because it wasn't deliberate.
It was just in trying to let the other by,
We'd blocked each other's way.
So he just laughs,
And he says – And *this* is what got me – He says,

One more time,
Then I really must go.

So I pass him by,
And off he strolls into his day.
But when I look back,
He's looking back too.
And the rest they say,
Is history.

A Man (*as he speaks he changes into jogging clothes, the same ones as in the footage*)
Saturday night,
Three am,

118   Once Upon a Bridge

Can't sleep with the noise.
There must have been a football match
Because the street below's aflow
With a river of wobbly legs,
Declaring victory for something
They played no actual part in.

I take a look across at the McDonald's
And it's absolutely hopping.
They must be playing The Bolero
Because there's a girl and guy,
Face to face,
Kneeling on the floor
Going right to left,
Left to right
Like that pair …
Torville and Dean.

He smiles, charmed by them.

They got the moves right.
Good for them.

Fully changed now, he turns to look at **A Woman**. *Their eyes meet for the first time.*

And I can't help but think of *her*,
The woman with no name,
And that day in May,
And how everything would be so different now,
If *I* had music in my ears,
Who knows where I'd be?
Garden,
Children,
Birthday clowns,
Rooftop terrace,
Overlooking Hampstead Heath,
Filling champagne flutes
And entertaining dinner guests with a curious tale,
Of how this one time on Putney Bridge,
I saw a woman come my way,
And before we passed into our day …

We briefly stopped
To dance.

Once Upon a Bridge   119

A Man *offers out a hand.*

We hear 'You'll Never Walk Alone' performed by Gerry and the Pacemakers.

A Woman *regards his outstretched hand, then reaches out her own. Then standing two metres apart, they assume a waltzing pose, then tenderly, tentatively, they begin a socially distanced waltz. As the song builds in momentum, the dance also builds in complexity as his desire for atonement grows along with her willingness to forgive him.*

As music ends, they separate and pass each other as they should have that morning on Putney Bridge, had circumstances been different.

The lights fade to black.

The End.

120   Once Upon a Bridge

Once Upon a Bridge was commissioned by Garry Hynes, Artistic Director of Druid Theatre in May of 2020. It was live streamed from the Mick Lally Theatre in Galway in February, 2021 with a subsequent 'watch on demand' run.

A note on the music

The music featured in the play is inspired by three moments during the coronavirus pandemic where people reached out in gestures of solidarity. With respect to future productions of this play, their contribution is essential to the tone of the drama. I wouldn't be inclined to change them.

Clair de Lune by Claude Debussy – one night in the early hours of the morning, pianist and composer Conor Linehan couldn't sleep so he got out of bed and filmed himself playing this piece of music for anyone who was having the same trouble.

You'll Never Walk Alone by Gerry and the Pacemakers – actor, Niall Buggy was filmed singing this iconic song of solidarity at the front gate of his home in Crouch End to the people passing by.

Whiter Shade of Pale by Procul Harum covered by Roland Alphonso – this was the first song DJ Donal Dineen played on *Make Me An Islander*, a weekly podcast with the mission of uniting the world through music.

A note on the footage

The actual footage of the incident that inspired the play is available on YouTube.

A note on the casting

To achieve the full dramatic impact at the end, I recommend the casting of **A Man** and **A Woman** be as close a mirror as possible to the figures in the footage. For **The Bus Driver**, I recommend looking up footage of Olivier Salbris for his tone and energy, which I think has huge value in telling this story.

A note on the story

Once Upon a Bridge is a work of fiction inspired by true events. Aside from the information taken from interviews given by the actual driver of Bus 430, the play is an act of the imagination. All three characters have been created from researching the lives of public transport workers, news articles, the response to the case on social media, talking to people about the footage, and hearing their stories about similar experiences.

The Last Return

Druid's world premiere production of *The Last Return* opened at Galway International Arts Festival in July 2022 before touring to Traverse Theatre for Edinburgh Festival Fringe (where it won a Scotsman Fringe First Award) and then to Dublin's Gate Theatre for Dublin Theatre Festival. In 2023, it toured Ireland, breaking Druid's box office records.

★★★★★ 'a true work of genius' – *The Times*
★★★★★ 'astonishingly original' – *What's On Stage*
★★★★★ 'blisteringly funny' – *The Arts Desk*

Galway International Arts Festival and Edinburgh Festival Fringe, 2022:

Cast

Umbrella Woman	**Fiona Bell**
Ticket Person	**Anna Healy**
Newspaper Man	**Bosco Hogan**
Military Man	**Fionn Ó Loingsigh**
Woman in Pink	**Naima Swaleh**

Creative Team

Writer	Sonya Kelly
Director	Sara Joyce
Set and Costume Design	Francis O'Connor
Lighting Design	Amy Mae
Sound Design & Composition	Michael John McCarthy
Movement	Jessica and Megan Kennedy (Junk Ensemble)
Dramatherapy	Wabriya King
Hair and Make-Up	Gráinne Coughlan
Associate Costume Designer	Clíodhna Hallissey
Assistant Director	Katie O'Halloran

Gate Theatre, Dublin Theatre Festival, 2022:

Cast

Umbrella Woman	**Rebecca O'Mara**
Ticket Person	**Anna Healy**
Newspaper Man	**Bosco Hogan**
Military Man	**Fionn Ó Loingsigh**
Woman in Pink	**Naima Swaleh**

Irish tour, 2023:

Cast

Umbrella Woman	**Rebecca O'Mara**
Ticket Person	**Anna Healy**
Newspaper Man	**Bosco Hogan**
Military Man	**Aidan Moriarty**
Woman in Pink	**Naima Swaleh**

The Last Return

For my parents, Veronica and Aidan Kelly,
watching from the stars

Characters

Ticket Person, *over thirty*
Newspaper Man, *over sixty*
Umbrella Woman, *over thirty*
Woman in Pink, *thirties / forties, Somali*
Military Man, *twenties, American*
Girl, *Somali*

A dash (–) suggests a beat, a new thought, a change in energy or atmosphere.

Curtains cloak the stage. Soothing classical music plays as the audience enter.

The house lights dip and we hear a gentle version of 'Anthem of Europe' ('Ode to Joy').

Est Europa nunc unita
Et unita maneat
Una in diversitate
Pacem mundi augeat
Semper regnant in Europa
Fides et iustitia
Et libertas populorum
In majore patria.
Cives, floreat Europa
Opus magnum vocat vos
Stellae signa sunt in caelo
Aureae, quae iungant nos.

The curtains open to reveal a theatre foyer.

US there is a ticket desk with a **Ticket Person** *working.*

Stage left there is a door over which a sign reads 'CAFÉ DOWNSTAIRS'.

There is a pay phone in an upstage corner. Downstage right of the ticket desk, a man with a newspaper sits on a stool doing the crossword.

There is a stool to his left with a backpack on it.

There are two stools in the upstage left corner, beside bucket and mop.

A woman with an umbrella enters as the final bars of music play. She is dressed as if she has come from the office and carries a largeish shoulder bag. She approaches the ticket desk and rings the bell. The **Ticket Person** *looks up.*

Umbrella Woman   Good evening.

Ticket Person   Hello.

Umbrella Woman   I would like to buy a ticket for tonight's performance of Oppenheimer's *Return to Hindenburg,* please.

Ticket Person   The Oppenheimer is sold out tonight.

Umbrella Woman   What?

Ticket Person   The Oppenheimer is sold out tonight.

Umbrella Woman   Oh dear. Oh no.

—

126   The Last Return

But tonight is Oppenheimer's final performance.

Ticket Person   Yes it is.

Umbrella Woman   And there are no tickets left?

Ticket Person   No.

Umbrella Woman   Are you sure?

Ticket Person   Yes I am.

Umbrella Woman   But I took two buses to get here. I was very much hoping to see it.

Ticket Person   Unfortunately all of the tickets are completely sold out.

Umbrella Woman   *Completely* sold out.

Ticket Person   That's what I said.

Umbrella Woman   Oh dear.

Ticket Person   Oppenheimer always sells out.

Umbrella Woman   Always?

Ticket Person   Always and completely.

Umbrella Woman   Oppenheimer must be very popular then.

Ticket Person   Extremely popular.

Umbrella Woman   I see.

—

And you are *absolutely* sure there are no tickets left?

Ticket Person   There are no tickets left. Absolutely.
I am sure.

Umbrella Woman   So there is *absolutely* no chance of my getting to see the Oppenheimer this evening then, is there?

Ticket Person   You can always wait, and if there are any last-minute returns, we will reissue the tickets ten minutes before the performance begins.

Umbrella Woman   Ah, so there is a good chance I *will* get a ticket.

Ticket Person   That's not what I said.

—

The Last Return   127

I said, there is a chance. If it is *good* chance or not, it is impossible to say. But you are here early and the weather forecast is inclement, which means some people may not show. So you might be in luck, you never know.

Umbrella Woman   Well, that is excellent news. Fingers crossed for inclement weather. My name is –

Ticket Person   We don't take names.

Umbrella Woman

–

Then may I take a number?

Ticket Person   We don't give out numbers.

Umbrella Woman   Then what is your system?

Ticket Person   You just have to wait in the queue.

Umbrella Woman   Wait in the queue?

Ticket Person   That's what I said.

Umbrella Woman   Where is the queue?

Ticket Person   The queue is over there.

Umbrella Woman   And which end is the end of the queue?

Ticket Person   I don't know. I am the ticket person, I am not responsible for organising the queue. It is up to the people in the queue to organise themselves.

Umbrella Woman   I see.

Ticket Person   All you have to do is place yourself after the last person who came in, and wait in the order in which you arrived. That is all. It's very simple really.

Umbrella Woman   All right.

–

In that case, I will find out for myself where the end of the queue is, place myself in the appropriate position, and wait my turn. Thank you.

Ticket Person   You're welcome.

The **Ticket Person** *returns to work. The* **Umbrella Woman** *approaches the* **Newspaper Man**.

128   The Last Return

Umbrella Woman   Excuse me, are you queuing for the Oppenheimer?

Newspaper Man   Yes.

Umbrella Woman   And is this the top of the queue or the bottom of the queue?

Newspaper Man   This is the top of the queue.

Umbrella Woman   Thank you.

Newspaper Man   You're welcome.

The **Umbrella Woman** *goes to the other end of the queue and stands beside the stool with the bag on it so the stool is positioned between them.*

They wait.

The **Umbrella Woman** *looks at the bag, looks at the* **Newspaper Man**, *looks away, looks at the bag, looks at the* **Newspaper Man**.

Umbrella Woman (*to* **Newspaper Man**)   Excuse me?

Newspaper Man   Yes?

Umbrella Woman   Is this your bag?

Newspaper Man   No.

They wait.

Umbrella Woman   Do you happen to know whom it belongs to?

Newspaper Man   It belongs to a girl in the café.

Umbrella Woman   A girl.

Newspaper Man   Yes.

Umbrella Woman   In the café.

Newspaper Man   Yes.

Umbrella Woman   I see.

—

Just checking.

—

And is she also queuing for the Oppenheimer?

Newspaper Man   She is.

Umbrella Woman   And the bag is there to mark her place.

Newspaper Man   Correct.

Umbrella Woman   And she asked you to mind it for her.

Newspaper Man   She did.

Umbrella Woman   I see.

—

How um ... long has she been gone for?

Newspaper Man   Oh about half an hour?

Umbrella Woman   Right.

They wait.

Newspaper Man   There are more stools over there if you want to sit down.

The **Umbrella Woman** *notices the stools for the first time.*

Umbrella Woman   Ah. So there are. If I go and get one, would you keep my place?

Newspaper Man   Certainly.

Umbrella Woman   Thank you.

The **Umbrella Woman** *gets a stool and returns.*

Umbrella Woman   Phew.

Sits.

I kept my place.

(*Soft joke.*) I owe you one.

Newspaper Man *smiles politely and does the crossword. The* **Umbrella Woman** *takes out a book. She opens it and reads.*

They wait.

Umbrella Woman (*little joke*)   Waiting: Fate's penance for the ill-prepared.

—

I took two buses to get here.

—

130   The Last Return

You?

Newspaper Man   Train.

Umbrella Woman   The person at the ticket desk said because of the weather there is a good chance of getting
a ticket.

—

Are you? Familiar? With Oppenheimer?

Newspaper Man   Yes.

He returns to the crossword.

Still, he can't resist the opportunity to show off his credentials.

Newspaper Man   I am a professor of Oppenheimer in fact.

Umbrella Woman   A *professor* of Oppenheimer? I say.

Newspaper Man   In fact I am leader in the field.

Umbrella Woman   Then you must be very familiar, I imagine.

Newspaper Man   I am very familiar, yes.

Umbrella Woman   Well, that is something. A *professor* of Oppenheimer. At where?

Newspaper Man   At the School of Oppenheimer.

Umbrella Woman   The *School* of Oppenheimer.

Newspaper Man   In the university.

Umbrella Woman   The *university*. Oppenheimer must be a truly great individual to warrant an entire school at a university.

Newspaper Man   Indeed.

Umbrella Woman   And how, in your opinion, Professor, can you tell if a person *is* truly great?

Newspaper Man   If you speak of a person by their first name only, and it is automatically understood whom it is you are speaking of, then that person is generally considered to be truly great.

Returns to crossword.

Umbrella Woman   Hm.

—

William.

Newspaper Man Shakespeare is one, yes.

Umbrella Woman –

Leonardo.

Newspaper Man Da Vinci is another, exactly.

Umbrella Woman –

Miranda.

Newspaper Man . . .

Umbrella Woman Ah, very good, I see your point.

–

Mirandas have a way to go.

–

So this particular Oppenheimer, I'm assuming you've seen it before?

Newspaper Man –

No.

Umbrella Woman Oh.

–

Leaving it a bit late are you not, for a man in your profession?

Newspaper Man Unfortunately, I have been unable to see it.

–

For health reasons.

–

I suffer from a condition that has … impeded my ability to sit for long periods of time without needing to use the gentlemen's facilities, which, given this theatre's policy of no re-admittance during the performance, has precluded me from seeing this production in its entirety.

Umbrella Woman Ah. That is a shame.

–

132   The Last Return

So you've *not* seen it then.

Newspaper Man   I have not seen *all* of it, no.

—

I have seen the beginning.

—

Thirty-seven times.

—

I have seen the beginning and middle, eleven times.

Umbrella Woman   And tonight I'll wager you are hoping to see the beginning, middle and end.

Newspaper Man   That is the plan.

Umbrella Woman   *If* you get a ticket.

Newspaper Man   Exactly.

Umbrella Woman   Which you will I am sure, as you are first in the queue.

—

Although I would have thought a person with your connections might have a few strings to pull.

Newspaper Man   At one time yes, I had a whole symphony of strings at my disposal. But now … There is a chance some sympathetic colleague from my department might call the ticket office and petition on my behalf, but it's slim.

—

Academia is cut-throat. People think it's all glowing pipes and corduroy trousers but it's not. The truth is, my position as head of the School of Oppenheimer *and* leader in the field is in grave jeopardy.

—

There are those among the outer, lesser, newer faculties who believe my teaching methods to have not, as they put it, 'moved with the times'. And so I am given to understand an unsavoury faction of dissenters is coalescing. No doubt they have the intention to see me deposed, and would gleefully interpret my failure to see this production as a sign of a much welcomed demise. A shot across the bows. A call to manoeuvre the troops, you might say. Then the vultures will circle. And as I turn my back to shoo one away, another will get closer.

—

That is how you slay a king: you move in increments. Subtle at first. A gentle touch on the wrist from a 'well-meaning colleague'. A good-natured enquiry after my health, and how it may be 'affecting my ability to execute my duties as leader in the field'. Then the rumour mill will start to grind its special blend of spices.

'Did you see him queuing for the Oppenheimer. Thirty-seven nights in a row.'

'I know. Oh, how sad.'

Next a private meeting of concerned parties will be held, followed by an extraordinary general meeting of the board, where no doubt the decision will be made that, due to 'essential cuts' and departmental restructuring, they will be forced to dissolve my position. Then the whole affair will be garnished with a carriage clock, a dribbling speech and the offer of a long sabbatical at some repugnant polytechnic. The chalk will be plucked from my hand. I will be carried off by my epaulettes and dumped at some joyless pile of breeze blocks beyond the bare horizon. Then some tight-cheeked, sharp-eyed, perky little bright spark will take my place, and before long my beloved School of Oppenheimer will be sliced and diced into an assortment of hideously titled sub- faculties, and my legacy will become nothing more than a footnote in some dusty periodical.

—

So you see, tonight, my situation is very desperate. I simply cannot fail.

Umbrella Woman   Well.

—

I am very sorry for your situation. It is hard to fathom what cruelties human beings are capable of.

Newspaper Man   Indeed.

The **Umbrella Woman**, *reaches into her bag, takes out a tin and opens it.*

Umbrella Woman   Would you like a protein ball?

—

134   The Last Return

They're homemade.

Newspaper Man   No, thank you.

The **Umbrella Woman** *puts the tin away.*

Umbrella Woman   And pardon my asking, Professor, how with your condition do you hope to get through this evening's performance without … being forced to leave the auditorium.

Newspaper Man   I have refrained from drinking liquids for the past twenty-four hours. I have also done my best to avoid stressful situations and certain triggers such as the mention or sound of running water.

Umbrella Woman   I see.

—

You must be very thirsty.

Newspaper Man   I am. And you?

Umbrella Woman   I had a cup of tea at lunch.

Newspaper Man   Have you seen this Oppenheimer before?

Umbrella Woman   Oh, yes.

—

Well, no. I have not seen it before, neither am I familiar with Oppenheimer at all, if truth be told.

—

I am familiar with the name, from colleagues at work. So you might say I know *of* Oppenheimer, but do not *know* know Oppenheimer … no … no …

—

I work in accounts.

—

The firm I work for was recently merged with an international group, and those of us who were kept on were forced to move to a rather inconvenient glass monstrosity up the river: open-plan office, bean bags, table tennis, all that nonsense. Anyway, it was quickly observed that the new head of HR had considerable sway in terms of promotions and demotions, if you get my drift. She swaggers in one morning and declares,

The Last Return   135

'I was at the Oppenheimer last night. Has anyone seen it? Oh you simply *have* to go.'

—

So one person did go, to get in with her – so to speak. Next thing, you know, he gets a corner office just like that. Glorious view. Personal fridge. Private coffee maker. All the comforts a person could want.

—

So naturally, seeing how this sudden affection for Oppenheimer was creating upward mobility among the barefoot ranks, one or two more people got tickets thinking, you know …

Points to ceiling as sign for promotion.

They too come skipping in declaring its restorative properties, and how it transformed their general world view. Next thing they're off on a golfing trip to the Caribbean. Luxury chalets. Pineapple cocktails. All expenses paid.

—

Next thing you know, people start to gather around the water filter at lunchtime to share quotes and jokes about the fabulous Oppenheimer, then they'd all high five each other and double up in fits of laughter all within earshot of 'you know who'. Laughter seasoned with a dash of something sinister: the venom of exclusion, you might say.

—

So as you can imagine the number of people who had seen the Oppenheimer begins to outweigh those who hadn't, at which time the quotes and jokes grow claws and barbs.

—

'What doesn't have a pulse and lives under a rock? Someone who hasn't been to the Oppenheimer! – Bah, ha, ha, ha, ha!'

Which becomes …

'*Not* been to the Oppenheimer? Well, she may as well go home and choke to death on her lasagne meal for one for all we care.'

Until then finally it's all …

136   The Last Return

'Oh don't ask *her* to the … drinks social or the team-building … paintballing excursion, or whatever. *She* hasn't seen the Oppenheimer.'

'Oh has she not? Well, she'd want to get her skates on because the season's nearly over, and no one round here wants to be lumped with, shackled to, marooned with the only person on the entire planet who hasn't bothered their backside to the Oppenheimer.'

Catches breath, calms.

So as a result, I am this evening hoping to become more familiar with Oppenheimer, on what appears to be my last opportunity to do so. And if I should fail, well … no doubt you can you can see my situation is equally desperate.

Newspaper Man (*returns to crossword*)   –

Well, fingers crossed for you.

Umbrella Woman   And fingers crossed for *you*. And legs too.

–

You were here last night, I take it?

Newspaper Man   I was.

Umbrella Woman   And you got in?

Newspaper Man   I did.

Umbrella Woman   Oh, good for you. Busy, was it?

Newspaper Man   There were ten of us waiting.

Umbrella Woman   *Ten*? And you all got tickets?

Newspaper Man   There were only two returns.

Umbrella Woman   Two you say?

Newspaper Man   Yes.

–

And the previous night there was only one.

They wait.

The **Umbrella Woman** *subtly counts on her fingers. She regards the bag. Her mood shifts.*

Umbrella Woman   Young, is she?

Newspaper Man   Hm?

Umbrella Woman   Young. Her in the café. I imagine she's a younger person.

Newspaper Man   Young. Yes. She is.

Umbrella Woman   And pretty.

Newspaper Man   Hm?

Umbrella Woman   Pretty big fan, of Oppenheimer, I'm thinking. I can tell by the type of bag. The bold choice of colours.

The **Newspaper Man** *returns to his crossword.*

Umbrella Woman   –

And her approach to the queueing system.

–

Because, well, it's not *really* queueing, is it? If you're not actually *in* the queue. That's what queueing is at the end of the day: the forfeiture of your freedom to multi-locate.

–

And if I may add, and I mean this with the greatest respect to you, Professor, but technically it was *not* you she should have asked to keep her place. Technically, she should have waited until a subsequent person had come along, and asked *them*. That would have been the decent thing to do. Because, surely the favour you ask is not of the person *ahead*, but the person who comes *after* you. Surely it is at *their* discretion to grant or deny permission to temporarily leave the queue. Because after all, it is not you she has put at a disadvantage. It is *me*. That's my thinking on it anyway.

The **Newspaper Man** *looks up, unable to avoid her any longer.*

Umbrella Woman   Not that I am any authority. That's just my own lowly interpretation of the rules.

Newspaper Man   Look –

Umbrella Woman   Not that I'm in charge of *making* the rules. I am merely a humble servant *to* them.

Newspaper Man   It's just … this being the last night –

Umbrella Woman   I know.

Newspaper Man   I'd rather not get involved –

Umbrella Woman   I understand.

Newspaper Man   I really need to keep my place.

Umbrella Woman   I am with you there one hundred per cent.

Newspaper Man   It's just too risky.

Umbrella Woman   I don't blame you.

Newspaper Man   I don't want to jeopardise my position –

Umbrella Woman   With so much at stake? Why would you?

Newspaper Man   Thanks. I don't want any unnecessary trouble –

Umbrella Woman   And bring on the urge to urinate, I completely understand.

–

Besides, why *should* you have to intervene? You are number one. You are king of the castle. *You* are at the top of the queue. Only a fool would pick sides in your position. It's not as if intervening is going to affect your chances. Should only one ticket become available, if you'll excuse the phrase, *you* are home and dry. So naturally, it is your privilege not to get involved with others less fortunate than yourself, the person the problem does not directly affect.

–

Even though it *was* you who instigated the chain of events by acquiescing to her request to sit in the café while also keeping her place in the foyer. I imagine, had you arrived second, and she was sitting in first place to your *right*, then skipped off for a big old feed, and popped herself back in *ahead* of you again, reeking of café au lait and quiche Lorraine, well then. I imagine you'd have had a lot to say under those conditions, particularly if only one ticket became available and she got in ahead of you, resulting in your academic career ending in disgrace. But, with the situation as it stands, if you'll pardon my reference to toilets and liquids, this is not your Waterloo.

The **Newspaper Man** *registers slight discomfort at the mention of water.*

The Last Return   139

Newspaper Man   Let's leave it at that, shall we?

Umbrella Woman   Yes.

—

Let's wash our hands of it.

The **Newspaper Man** *returns to his crossword. The* **Umbrella Woman** *reads her book.*

They wait.

The **Umbrella Woman** *checks her watch and looks at the bag again.*

Umbrella Woman   Tell you what, I am quite skilled at navigating these situations. Why don't I pop to the desk and have a word with the ticket person, who looks like a reasonable type and might settle the situation. Would you watch my seat?

Newspaper Man (*reluctant*)   Fine.

Umbrella Woman *puts away her book and approaches the* **Ticket Person**. *She rings the bell.*

Umbrella Woman (*to* **Ticket Person**)   Excuse me?

Ticket Person   Hello.

Umbrella Woman   Yes, hello –

Ticket Person   The Oppenheimer is sold out tonight.

Umbrella Woman   I know –

Ticket Person   If you want to wait for a last-minute return, please join the queue and we will reissue the tickets ten minutes before the performance begins.

Umbrella Woman   Yes, I already did that. In fact I did exactly as you instructed. But there's this young lady, see – if going by her actions, you can call her that – she left her bag on that stool there to keep her place in the queue, and absconded to the café.

She has now been gone for at least half an hour, possibly more, which in my understanding of fairness and decency does not constitute a respectful attitude to those who are queueing in the normal manner. Instead, she is –

Ticket Person   Madam –

Umbrella Woman – in there, no doubt stuffing her face with Weiner schnitzel –

Ticket Person Madam –

Umbrella Woman – or some such other highly processed pig product while we, the common decent people, are forced to –

Ticket Person I am the ticket person, madam.

Umbrella Woman Yes, yes, I know, but –

Ticket Person I am not charged with arbitrating matters pertaining to the order of the queue, its configuration and how you perceive it to be corrupted. I believe you were furnished with this information when you came in.

Umbrella Woman I know I was, but this is an emergency –

Ticket Person No it is not.

Umbrella Woman It is actually. It's an emergency to me, and I wouldn't normally intervene but –

Ticket Person Madam, I am the ticket person.

Umbrella Woman So you keep saying.

Ticket Person I do not organise the ticket queue, it is up to the people in the ticket queue to organise themselves. Have I made myself clear?

Umbrella Woman –

You're the ticket person.

Ticket Person Correct.

Umbrella Woman You sell the tickets.

Ticket Person Yes.

Umbrella Woman Answer the phone.

Ticket Person Yes.

Umbrella Woman Tell people the Oppenheimer is sold out tonight, wait over there, you might get a ticket if it rains.

Ticket Person Yes.

Umbrella Woman –

Not exactly aiming high in life, are you? If that's *all* you do.

Ticket Person   It is not, as a matter of fact, *all* I do.

Umbrella Woman   Oh, what else then? Polish your staple gun? Measure your paperclips?

Ticket Person (*gesturing to phone*)   I am also trained to use this hotline to report code red situations detailed in this catalogue, such as fire, robbery, medical emergencies, suspicious persons or items, terrorist attacks, anyone brandishing a weapon, blunt, sharp, semi or fully automatic, *and* remove from the building any person who behaves in an insulting or confrontational manner to any member of staff. Do I make myself clear?

Umbrella Woman   –

Oh, you mean me. But I am not being insulting and confrontational, I am merely the victim of someone who is. And as a passport-holding, tax-paying citizen born of this nation, I am requesting intervention from a representative of one of its national institutions. Furthermore, I demand some act –

The **Ticket Person** *lifts the red phone's receiver.*

Umbrella Woman   Wh … what are you doing?

The **Ticket Person** *dials.*

Umbrella Woman   No, no, I am the decent person here. She –

Ticket Person   Hello, security –

Umbrella Woman   Wait! Yes! Clear! Crystal clear. As a mountain spring in summertime.

The **Ticket Person** *puts down the phone.*

Umbrella Woman   You have been firm and clear. I respect that in a person. You are a role model to us all. Sorry to have troubled you. Apologies for the inconvenience, and for compromising your professional aptitude, and ridiculing your life goals. Thank you for your time.

Bows.

Ticket Person   You're welcome.

The **Ticket Person** *returns to work.*

Umbrella Woman (*backing away to her seat*)   Had I arrived before the man with the newspaper over there, who messed the whole thing up by

142 The Last Return

lacking the courage to say no to an unreasonable request, I would never have bothered you in the first place.

(*Looking at* **Newspaper Man**.) And they call *us* the weaker sex.

The **Umbrella Woman** *sits and regards the* **Newspaper Man** *coldly.*

Newspaper Man (*not sorry*)   Sorry I couldn't help.

–

Only … tonight is my –

Umbrella Woman (*cool*)   Last chance, you said, I know.

Newspaper Man   My situation is very desperate, I cannot get involved.

Umbrella Woman   'S fine. Don't worry.

The **Newspaper Man** *hides in his crossword.*

The **Umbrella Woman** *takes a clear plastic litre bottle of mineral water out of her bag. She ceremoniously unscrews it, leans and looks over the* **Newspaper Man***'s shoulder.*

Umbrella Woman   Ten across. Pour downwards rapidly and in large quantities.

(*Muses.*) Cascade.

She takes large gulp of water, swishes it lavishly between her teeth and cheeks, gargles loudly and swallows with relish, much to the **Newspaper Man***'s discomfort.*

Umbrella Woman   Ahhhhhh.

Sudden thunder, the sound of rain, a flash of lightning and another clap of thunder, plunging the foyer into a few seconds of darkness, which, when subsided, reveals a woman in a pink head scarf or hijab at the entrance to the foyer. She carries a bag of belongings. The rain ebbs. She approaches the **Ticket Person** *and rings the bell.*

Ticket Person   Good evening.

The **Woman in Pink** *takes out her phone, presses play and extends it towards the* **Ticket Person***.*

Pink Phone   Excuse. Me. I. Would. Like. Some. Informations. Is this the. Place. Where. There. Is. A performance. Of. Oppenheimer's. Return. To. Hindenburg. Please.

The **Ticket Person** *disappears under her desk, reappears with a pointer stick and hands it to the* **Woman in Pink**. *The* **Ticket Person** *pulls a chord and a giant map of the world comes down like a roller blind. The* **Woman in Pink** *points to Somalia.*

The **Ticket Person** *checks the map, puts it away, retrieves the pointer stick and puts it away, and re-emerges with a cassette player and a cassette, puts it in the machine and presses play.*

Machine (*in Italian*)   *Sì. Esso. È. Tuttavia. Il. Oppenheimer. È. Venduto. Fuori. Stasera. Puoi. Sempre. Attesa. In. Il. Coda. Al di sopra di. Là. E. Se. Là. Sono. Qualunque. Scorso. Minuto. Ritorna. Noi. Volere. Ristampa. Loro. Dieci minuti prima. Il inizia la performance.* (Yes. It. Is. However. The. Oppenheimer. Is. Sold. Out. Tonight. You can. Always. Wait. In. The. Queue. Over. There. And. If. There. Are. Any. Last. Minute. Returns. We. Will. Reissue. Them. Ten minutes before. The performance begins.)

The **Ticket Person** *presses stop. The* **Woman in Pink** *presses her phone.*

Pink Phone   *Prego.* (Thank you.)

The **Ticket Person** *presses play.*

Machine (*in Italian*)   You're welcome.

The **Ticket Person** *puts the recorder away and returns to work.*

The **Woman in Pink** *coolly surveys the terrain. She goes to the upper stage left corner, picks up the remaining stool and looks at the queue, deciding which end to sit at. She walks towards the* **Umbrella Woman**'s *end but then veers towards the* **Newspaper Man***, sits beside him and calmly occupies herself with her phone.*

The **Newspaper Man** *is unsure how to handle it. The* **Umbrella Woman** *smiles smugly.*

They wait.

Umbrella Woman (*to the* **Newspaper Man**)   How many returns did you say there were last night, Professor?

Newspaper Man   Two.

Umbrella Woman   And how many the night before?

The **Newspaper Man** *subtly counts on his fingers. The answer dawns on him. He looks at the* **Woman in Pink***, then back again.*

144   The Last Return

Umbrella Woman   As a fellow citizen I felt a duty to point it out. But perhaps I should not have raised the matter, in light of how adamantly you expressed your wish 'not to get involved'.

Newspaper Man (*turning to the* **Woman in Pink**)   Excuse me, are you queueing for the Oppenheimer? Because if you are, you're at the wrong end of the queue and you're going to have to move.

The **Woman in Pink** *smiles at him graciously and goes back to her phone.*

Newspaper Man   There's a queue you see? You know – a queue? This end of the queue is not the end of the queue. The end of the queue is down there. After her. She is number three. I am number one and you are number four. Four.

—

Me one. You four.

Umbrella Woman   She doesn't understand you.

Newspaper Man   She doesn't understand what I'm saying.

Umbrella Woman   *Me one. You four.* Really, Professor, is that the best you can do?

Newspaper Man   Then what do you suggest?

Umbrella Woman   Why don't you try asking the ticket person for assistance in the matter?

Newspaper Man   If I do that would you mind my place?

Umbrella Woman   It would be my pleasure to return the favour.

The **Newspaper Man** *puts his paper and pen on his seat and approaches the* **Ticket Person**. *He rings the bell.*

Newspaper Man   Excuse me?

Ticket Person   Good evening.

Newspaper Man   Hello.

Ticket Person   The Oppenheimer is sold out tonight.

Newspaper Man   I know.

Ticket Person   If you want, you can queue for a last-minute return and we will reissue the tickets ten minutes before the performance begins.

The Last Return   145

Newspaper Man   Actually, I'm already in the queue. I'm number one, in fact, but there was a lady in pink who approached you a minute ago, she's come over and sat down at the wrong end of the queue and –

Ticket Person   I do not intervene on matters regarding the queue, sir. It is up to the members of the queue to organise themselves.

Newspaper Man   I know. I respect your position and wouldn't dream of asking you to intervene. In fact, I am perfectly capable of handling the situation myself. But to safeguard against any unintended affront, I just need to know what language she speaks.

–

You had some sort of system whereby you made it possible to communicate.

Ticket Person   We don't keep that information on record.

Newspaper Man   But it was just a minute ago. She pointed at a map. You played a cassette. Surely you must recall the country and the language.

Ticket Person   The countries are colour coded, sir, as are the cassettes.

Newspaper Man   I see.

Ticket Person   I select the cassette in accordance with its corresponding country colour code, as identified by the customer.

Newspaper Man   Right.

Ticket Person   That is the system. It is designed to protect the staff from displaying any unconscious bias that may offend the customers' national, cultural and racial heritage, which in some cases can differ in all three categories.

Newspaper Man   Right.

Ticket Person   If the system gets it wrong, and the customer is offended, then it is the system's fault, not the staff member's. It was introduced after the O'Flanagan versus Takahashi case, when a cloakroom attendant mistakenly addressed a Japanese person in Mandarin, resulting in the invasion of Manchuria in 1945.

Newspaper Man   I see.

–

146   The Last Return

A little antiquated, is it not? Your system.

Ticket Person   Do you wish to file a complaint against the system?

Newspaper Man   No, but going by what I *think* I heard, she's Italian. *Is* she Italian?

Ticket Person   She may be Italian. She may not be Italian. Either way, it's not my fault.

Newspaper Man   Right. Well. Thank you. That's been ... most helpful.

Ticket Person   You're welcome.

The **Ticket Person** *returns to work. The* **Newspaper Man** *returns to his seat.*

They wait.

Umbrella Woman   Italian?

Newspaper Man   Italian. I think.

Umbrella Woman   Do you have a device to translate?

Newspaper Man   No. Do you?

Umbrella Woman   But of course. I move with the times.

Newspaper Man   Then would you ...?

The **Umbrella Woman** *tactically returns to her book.*

Newspaper Man   Correct me if I am wrong, but earlier, when you came in, you had no stool to sit on.

Umbrella Woman   That is correct.

Newspaper Man   And I said, 'There's some over there, if you want to sit down.' And you said, 'Oh, if I go and get one, would you mind to keep my place?' And I said, 'Sure, no problem. I would be delighted, to do that favour for you. Anything to help a stranger.'

Umbrella Woman   Something to that effect.

Newspaper Man   And you said, 'Thanks. I owe you one.'

Umbrella Woman   I did.

—

And when you went up to the ticket person just now, you said, 'I beseech you dear lady, would you please mind my place?' And I said, ' Certainly. It would be my pleasure to return the favour.' Which I did. Successfully. So now we are even.

Newspaper Man   I accept your point. However, should this woman choose to elbow in ahead of me when the last returns are released, she will have elbowed in ahead of all of us and, in so doing, deliver an ever diminishing outcome of success to each subsequent queuer. Such is the unfortunate knock-on effect of her decision to sit where she sat. Then *you* will be pushed into number four, and if only three returns become available, you will be left without a ticket.

Umbrella Woman (*getting up*)   Italian, you said.

The **Umbrella Woman** *approaches the* **Woman in Pink**, *gets her phone out and types. She presses play.*

The **Newspaper Man** *conveniently occupies himself with his crossword during the exchange.*

Umbrella Phone (*in Italian*)   *Scusa. Me. Sei. Italiano?* (Excuse. Me. Are. You. Italian?)

The **Woman in Pink** *types.*

Pink Phone (*in English*)   No. I. Am. Not. Italian. I. Am. Somali. But I. Understand. Italian.

Umbrella Phone   My. Apologies.

Pink Phone   No need to. Apologise. The ticket person. Got it wrong. Somalia was briefly under Italian rule. And the translation system she is using. Has post-colonial biases.

Umbrella Phone   I understand. And tell me, are you queueing for the Oppenheimer?

Pink Phone   I am waiting. For someone.

Umbrella Woman   You're waiting for someone?

Pink Phone   I am. Waiting. For someone.

Umbrella Woman   Oh I see. So you're *not* queueing for the Oppenheimer then?

Pink Phone   I am. Waiting. For someone.

148   The Last Return

Umbrella Woman   Then you're not ... here to ...

Pink Phone   I am. Waiting. For someone.

Umbrella Woman   You're waiting for someone. I *see. We* thought you were trying to ... you know – because there's a queue you see –

Pink Phone   I am. Waiting. For someone.

Umbrella Woman   Yes, yes, you said. That's fine. Well then in that case ...

Umbrella Phone   Thank you.

The **Woman in Pink** *gives her a flat smile and returns to her phone. The* **Umbrella Woman** *returns to her seat.*

The **Newspaper Man** *looks up from his paper.*

Umbrella Woman (*to* **Newspaper Man**)   It's fine, she says she's not queueing to see the Oppenheimer, she's just waiting for someone.

Newspaper Man   She's waiting for someone.

Umbrella Woman   Yes.

Newspaper Man   Who?

Umbrella Woman   I don't know.

Newspaper Man   But she is waiting for someone?

Umbrella Woman   Yes.

Newspaper Man   You sure?

Umbrella Woman   I am.

Newspaper Man   You're absolutely sure?

Umbrella Woman   Yes absolutely I am sure. Whom she is waiting for is immaterial. What matters is her presence in the queue does not affect our own circumstances. That's *all* we need to know.

Newspaper Man   Right. It's just sometimes people come in pretending to 'escape the rain', or they need to 'rest their feet', or they're 'waiting for a friend' but it's really just a trick to jump to the top of the queue. But as you say if you're absolutely sure –

Umbrella Woman   Unequivocally. I am sure. And in light of your failure to successfully investigate the situation, I will thank you not to doubt my efforts.

The pay phone rings. No one moves.

Umbrella Woman   Might that be your cavalry?

Newspaper Man   Hm?

Umbrella Woman   You mentioned earlier there was a chance a sympathetic colleague might call the ticket office and pull a few strings.

Newspaper Man   Oh yes! Yes, yes, yes. If I go, will you mind my seat?

Umbrella Woman   You want me, who is third, to keep your place for you, who is first, while you see if you can organise a ticket for yourself, and if you can't, you just come back and be first again? Want me to do anything else for you? Vacuum your living room? Iron your shirts?

Newspaper Man   But you were the one who said it might be for me –

Umbrella Woman   Let me think.

Newspaper Man (*getting fraught*)   Please.

Umbrella Woman   It's just it'll be the second favour I'll have done for you since I got here, and I'm starting to feel my good will has been somewhat overstretched.

Newspaper Man   But my situation is desperate.

Umbrella Woman   As is mine.

Newspaper Man   Please.

—

If it's good news, you can have my place in the queue.

Umbrella Woman   And the bag-dumping, queue-jumping, pork guzzler in the café will remain second?

Newspaper Man   Yes.

Umbrella Woman   And I will be first.

Newspaper Man   Yes.

Umbrella Woman   Deal.

150   The Last Return

The **Umbrella Woman** *gives a grudging nod towards the phone by way of permission. The* **Newspaper Man** *rushes to answer it.*

Newspaper Man   Hello? Are you from the university? The line is very poor. Can you repeat that please?

The **Umbrella Woman** *looks at the* **Woman in Pink**.

Umbrella Woman   No sign of your friend yet. Hopefully you won't be waiting too long.

The **Woman in Pink** *gives a polite smile. The* **Umbrella Woman** *takes out her tin and offers a protein ball to the* **Woman in Pink**, *who thinks, then cautiously accepts one. The* **Umbrella Woman** *watches, waiting for her to eat it. The* **Woman in Pink** *puts it in her pocket. The* **Umbrella Woman** *puts the tin away. They both turn and gaze ahead.*

Suspicion descends.

Umbrella Woman   I would like to tell you a little story if I may, about a train trip I made in my youth from Saint Petersburg to Passchendaele. We stopped at the city of Passau. A man came on board. He occupied the seat beside me, placing his elbow on the armrest between us, as was his right to do so. Still, having had the armrest all to myself for several hundred miles, I felt more entitled to it than he, so I elbowed him off, taking more than my share. When he petitioned me to co-occupy the armrest equally, I pretended I didn't understand a word he said. The language barrier tactic, I believe it's called. I regret that now.

—

It is a common phenomenon in densely populated cities such as this to encounter those who prefer to deceive strangers for profit rather than seek their fortune by fair means. As insignificant as these misdemeanours may seem, they build up. And up and up and up and up until soon we are no longer a society of civic-minded people who pull together for the common good, but an individuated mass of self-serving globules clamouring over each other for personal gain. Systems collapse. Chaos prevails. Tyranny takes hold. Then next thing you know … well, I refer you to the last four hundred years of European history, where the lines of our nations were drawn with the blood of the innocent, and were by their very nature the Armrests of Shame.

They eye each other intensely as in a stand-off. The **Woman in Pink** *coolly puts in her headphones (the international symbol for 'I am no longer available for further communication') and returns to her phone.*

The Last Return   151

Newspaper Man (*to pay phone*)   Can you understand me? Did. You. Hear. What. I. Said.

Thunder, lightning and the pulse of rain.

The foyer doors burst open. A **Military Man** *enters, wet from his travels. He wears an air-force fly suit, a headset and maybe a helmet or a cap. Perhaps he is decorated with medals. He walks up to the ticket desk with an affable air of confidence that masks a burning inner crisis. He rings the bell. The* **Ticket Person** *turns.*

Ticket Person   Good evening.

Military Man (*taking out wallet*)   Good evening.

If you please, I'd like to buy a ticket for the Oppenheimer show.

Ticket Person   The Oppenheimer is sold out tonight.

Military Man   It's what?

Ticket Person   Sold out.

Military Man   Sold out?

Ticket Person   That's what I said.

Military Man   The Oppenheimer's sold out tonight. God damn it no! It can not be true!

The **Military Man** *falls to his knees. He is distraught.*

Ticket Person   I'm afraid it can because it is.

Military Man   Goddamnit. Damnit. Damnit. Damn, damn, damn. Are you sure?

Ticket Person   I am. Absolutely.

Military Man   It's just, you don't understand. I gotta see this show.

Newspaper Man (*to phone*)   Are. You. From. The. Uni.Ver. Sity?

Military Man   I mean I really *have* to see it. I *absolutely* have to. Isn't there anything you can do?

Ticket Person   If you want, you can queue over there for a last-minute return and we will reissue the tickets ten minutes before the performance begins..

Military Man   And you'll sell me a ticket then?

Ticket Person   That depends.

152   The Last Return

Military Man   On what?

Newspaper Man   Are you my cavalry?

Ticket Person   On how many tickets become available and how many people are waiting.

Newspaper Man   Because if you are not, I need to go back to my place in the queue.

The **Military Man** *gets off the floor.*

Military Man   Okay, that's good news. Phew! I'll take my chances in the line. Thank you so much. Thank you.

Ticket Person   You're welcome.

The **Ticket Person** *returns to work.*

The **Military Man** *looks at the queue, makes a decision and approaches the* **Woman in Pink**.

Military Man   Excuse me, ma'am, is this the line for the Oppenheimer show?

The **Woman in Pink** *ignores him.*

Umbrella Woman   Hello, sir. May I help?

Military Man (*to* **Umbrella Woman**)   Yes. I need to know is this the line for the Oppenheimer show?

Umbrella Woman   The *queue* – Yes it is but she's not queueing.

Military Man   O-kay.

Umbrella Woman   She's just come in to wait for someone.

Military Man   And you, ma'am, are you in the line?

Umbrella Woman   The *queue* – yes I am the last person. Number three.

Military Man   Number three?

Umbrella Woman   A girl down in the café is number two. She has left her bag here to mark her place – which isn't really queuing is it? – but the man in that seat there gave her permission. I've heard she's an absolute weapon, but I daren't intervene as he is number one, not me.

Military Man   And where is he?

Umbrella Woman   Over there on the phone trying to secure a ticket through a tenuous back channel and *will* return to his seat if he is unsuccessful.

Military Man   And that's okay with you?

Umbrella Woman   Well, no … but if he is successful, it is agreed that I will move to number one, in exchange for minding his seat, in light of the girl in the café's absence and subsequent relegation from the negotiations thereof, thus elevating you to the position of number three in place of me being number one.

Military Man   So in the meantime, *you* are number three and *I* am number four.

Umbrella Woman   Correct.

Military Man   Holy cow.

He glances about for a seat.

Umbrella Woman   If it's a stool you're after, you are out of luck as the girl in the café who is not even queuing has annexed that one for her bag.

Military Man   Well, in that case, do you think he'll mind if I sit in his seat for a while? I've come such a long way and if truth be told, I'm a little pooped.

Umbrella Woman   Em …

Military Man   When he comes back, I'll move down there to where I'm supposed to go.

Umbrella Woman   If it doesn't affect the ultimate outcome, what's the harm?

Military Man (*sitting*)   Exactly.

Newspaper Man (*shouting into phone*)   That's it! I am reporting you to your head of department. Right now.

The **Newspaper Man** *hangs up and fishes for coins in his pockets. He makes a call.*

Umbrella Woman   I took two buses to get here.

—

You?

154   The Last Return

Military Man   Flew.

Umbrella Woman   Ooh. Fast.

Military Man   Not fast enough to get here first.

Smiles.

Newspaper Man   Hello. Put me through to Women's Studies please.

Military Man   Some crazy system you people got set up here I have to say.

Umbrella Woman   Believe me, things would be very different if I had gotten here first.

The **Umbrella Woman** *nods towards the* **Newspaper Man** *as an indication of blame.*

Military Man   What's his deal?

Umbrella Woman (*hush hush*)   He's ill. Incontinence due to stress in the workplace. So whatever you do, do not under any circumstances mention anything to do with the old H_2O. Taps, rivers, lakes, toilets, aqueducts, waterfalls. Any reference to fluids could set him off to the bathroom and jeopardise his place.

Military Man   O-kay …

Umbrella Woman   His job is on the line. It's driven him half mad. If he doesn't get in tonight, it's curtains. Sad, is it not? How the mind can turn to soup.

Military Man   You don't have to tell me. I'm here on doctor's orders.

—

I saw action.

The **Umbrella Woman** *is transfixed.*

Umbrella Woman   War.

Military Man   Uh-huh.

Umbrella Woman   Where?

Military Man   Can't say.

Umbrella Woman   With who?

Military Man   I don't know. But I do know this. A year ago I was just another dead-beat drop-out kid from a one-horse town with a one-way ticket to nowhere fast. The town factory shut, the bank foreclosed, my mom lost all her savings to a subprime loan. She turned to opioids for company, and shoot 'em up computer games was the only life I knew.

One night down the video arcade I was riding high on Jungle Strike. Just topped the leader board fourth time in a row. Pee-ome! Peome! Peome! Flying up above the badlands six hundred feet below, fingers dancing on the trigger keys like frickin' Fred Astaire.

Peome!

My mission: to stop Ibn Kilbaba, the evil warlord's plot to blow up Washington, DC. Peome! Peome! Peome!

Take that, you evil warlord. Run if you want, you'll only die tired. Peome! Peome-peome-peome!

Ibn Kilbaba, you exit the game! And when I hit that top score, man, the whole arcade was screaming out my name.

'Dude! You are king of the strip mall, man! Go get this kid a soda pop!'

Then all at once, a hand came on my shoulder and a voice came in my ear, and I swear to God it could've been the father I never knew.

'See that guy you're shooting, son? Come with me today and you can shoot that guy for real.'

So they signed me in, trained me up and shipped me to their German air base for immediate active duty. Zero to hero in six months flat. Next thing I know I'm in mission control, flying RPAs over desert sands ten thousand miles away, coasting high above the mountains of the Hindu Kush, soaring past the pirate ships of the Arabian Sea down to where the Gulf of Aden meets the Horn of Africa.

A sharp rumble of thunder ruptures the air.

Without even lifting her head, the **Woman in Pink***'s eyes shoot up from her phone at the mention of her homeland. She coolly stares ahead.*

Military Man   Two thumbs poised to rid the world of evil with a click. 'Target identified. Prepare to engage.' And there he is: Evil Kilbaba, like in the video arcade back home. Just another greasy little dirt ball in the crosshairs of my screen.

Then click! Splash! Peome! Peome! Peome!

156   The Last Return

Up he goes in a crimson plume of metal, blood and bone. Target neutralised.

You exit the game.

—

'Good job, son.'

I hit thirteen targets in a week, sixty in a month and I am top of the leader board in the greatest video game on earth.

—

One day we tracked this target up a dirt road, though the backyard of a house. Real bad guy. Ibn Kilbaba maybe times ten. So I sit real still, ready for the strike, sweat pooling in the sockets of my eyes, fingers still as stone. Waiting for the order to whisper in my ear.

Assumes position with thumbs.

And then I see her.

—

Coming out the backdoor towards the gate, feet pumping up the dust as she breaks into a run, hands reaching upwards, outwards, toward his face. Just a little girl running to her daddy when she sees him coming home.

'Daaaadeeeee.'

'Target clear. Prepare to engage.' 'Daaaadeeeee.'

'No ... no, no! She's in the line of fire. Move out of there! Move out! If I splash him now, she'll get it too, and I can't do that, no way.'

So I say, 'Negative, sir! There's a kid in the yard.' 'Negative, son. You are clear to engage.'

'Negative, sir. There's a kid in the yard. It's a little girl. I can see her, clear as day.' 'It's a dog,' they said.

'It's not a dog.'

'It's a dog,' they said.

'It's not a dog.'

'It's a dog,' they said, 'looking for its bone. Now do your fucking duty, son, so we can all go home.'

The **Military Man** *stares in horror at his thumbs, raised in the air in front of him. We hear a single distant rumble of thunder, not unlike an explosion, as they press down on the imaginary trigger underneath.*

Military Man   'Good job, son. Go get this kid a beer.'

—

I get out of my chair, head for home, turn out the light, lay on the bed and there she was, the little desert girl, hands stretching upwards, outwards towards my face. I shut my eyes and plug my ears just in case I hear the words come out her mouth …

Softly calls.

'Daaaadeeeeeeeee …'

Puts thumbs down.

They put me on Ambien to sleep. Dexadrine to wake. Aderal for pain. Serequell for nerves. Electroshock, cerebral probe, micro dose. They tried it all but they didn't have a drill or pill to make her go away. And every night, without fail, she'd come out to play, climbing up the walls, sliding down the sand dunes in my brain.

I thought, I can't go on like this, I'd rather die. Shrink said, 'Well, there's only one thing left to do then, son. You gotta get a ticket to the Oppenheimer show. It will shine a light so bright, you will see it from another galaxy, as if a thousand suns set fire to your pain.'

(*Tearful.*) And now tonight's my only chance. So my situation's pretty desperate, can't you see? I gotta see this show.

Umbrella Woman   Desperate, yes, indeed. You poor dear man. After all you've sacrificed, an evening at the theatre is the very least you deserve.

The **Umbrella Woman** *is about to go to her bag but is distracted by the* **Newspaper Man**.

Newspaper Man   Well, if Gertrude won't come to the phone, you can tell her from me, I will not be intimidated by her battalion of hairy-legged, uni-browed, brassiere burning parasites. I am first in the queue tonight. I *will* see this production. So you can *take* your carriage clock and stick it where Apollo's sun has yet to set.

The **Newspaper Man** *slams down the phone. He turns and sees his seat has been taken. His face darkens with rage.*

158   The Last Return

Newspaper Man   Well, heavens to Betsy, what have we here?

The **Newspaper Man** *approaches.*

Newspaper Man (*to* **Military Man**)   You! Get off my chair!

Military Man (*to* **Umbrella Woman**)   I'll handle this.

The **Military Man** *attempts to rise. The* **Umbrella Woman**
stops him.

Umbrella Woman (*to* **Military Man**)   I'll handle this.

Newspaper Man (*to* **Umbrella Woman**)   I knew it! I knew better
than to trust you.

Umbrella Woman (*eyes on* **Newspaper Man**)   Ah, I see having failed
in your efforts to secure a ticket through collegial pity, *and* seeing someone
in your seat on your return, you have leapt to conclusions about our
agreement to hold to your place, which I had no obligation to honour, but
did so out of the goodness of my own heart. This young man is a war
hero, and has merely borrowed your seat as he was tired.

Military Man   I just needed to rest my feet.

Newspaper Man (*to* **Umbrella Woman**)   Bah! I warned you that's a
trick. You fool! Did you not listen after everything I did for you?

Umbrella Woman   After everything you did for me? You
disenfranchised me from my rightful place as number two before I even
got here.

Newspaper Man   I did no such thing! I could tell the minute you
walked in you were going to be trouble, with your super-saccharine please
and thank yous and, and, and your face like a chewed grapefruit.

Military Man   Whoa there!

Newspaper Man (*to* **Military Man**)   Don't you whoa me, Sonny Jim.
I am not a horse!

The **Newspaper Man** *squares up to the* **Umbrella Woman**.

Newspaper Man (*re: phone*)   Come on, who sent you? Who from that
petri dish of confused zygotes up in Gender Studies put you up to this?
Was it Gertrude? Was it Claribel? Was it Mildred? Was it Jane?

Umbrella Woman   Careful now, don't stress yourself. You might
spring a leak and miss the show.

Military Man   Wait, wait, wait, let me get this straight, I am number three and you are number two. Is that correct?

Umbrella Woman   No. I am number three and you are number four. That ineffectual pile of corduroy is number one, the pig-eating psycho he allowed to sit in the café is number two, and the woman in pink has nothing to do
with it.

Newspaper Man   This woman, if you can call her that, has been trying to trick me out of my seat ever since she came in and is no doubt using you for the purpose.

Umbrella Woman   I am doing no such thing you dribbley-cocked milksop.

Military Man (*to* **Umbrella Woman**)   You've put up with enough. Let me handle this.

(*Standing, to* **Newspaper Man**.) Sir, you need to calm down and take back your rightful seat.

Newspaper Man   What?

Military Man   Take your seat. Take it.

Newspaper Man   Take it?

Umbrella Woman   You heard the man. Take your precious seat before this whole situation gets blown out of the water and bursts completely out of control …

Newspaper Man   Ooh …

The **Newspaper Man** *needs the bathroom.*

The **Umbrella Woman** *sees his predicament and enjoys the power she wields over him …*

Umbrella Woman   Yes … like a tsunami, or a great big aqueduct ready to overflow, spilling all kinds of half truths, and flooding the sitation with nonsense until we are all simply floating down a river of madness to an ocean of despair.

Newspaper Man   Ahhh …

Umbrella Woman   This reminds me of the time I went fishing out on the lake –

160   The Last Return

The **Newspaper Man** *is about to explode.*

Newspaper Man   Please ... no more.

Military Man   Are you okay, sir? Please sit down.

Newspaper Man (*about to sit*)   Actually ... I have to pop to the bathroom for a minute. I feel a bit –

Military Man   Sure thing. When you gotta go, you gotta go.

Newspaper Man   Could I trouble you to keep my place?

Military Man   Not a problem.

Newspaper Man   Only I'm afraid that she might –

Military Man   Trust me, it's all under control, sir.

Newspaper Man   Thank you ...

Military Man (*giving jovial salute*)   Ten four. Reporting for duty. Your seat is safe with me, sir.

The **Newspaper Man** *returns the salute and exits. The* **Military Man**'s *charm slides as he watches him go. He retakes the stool and checks his watch.*

They wait.

Military Man   So *that's* the guy who set up this whole system?

Umbrella Woman   Yes. Did you see the way he went for me?

Military Man   Sure did.

Umbrella Woman   Well done, by the way, keeping your cool.

Military Man   Conflict resolution. It's part of my training.

—

So what are our chances of getting a ticket? As they stand.

Umbrella Woman   After him in the bathroom and her in the café, slim I'd say at most.

Military Man   Slim.

Umbrella Woman   Yes. Mine, obviously a little less so than yours. But that's the luck of the draw I suppose, given the order in which we arrived.

Military Man   Yep.

That's the luck of the draw. I guess.

They wait.

And at least now, you have nothing to worry about, if you come under attack again. You're totally safe with me in charge.

Umbrella Woman Hm?

Military Man You don't have to worry. With me in charge. I'll handle things from here on out. It's for the best.

Umbrella Woman Oh really there really is no need for that.

Military Man Oh, ma'am, I really think there is.

(Clarifying.) Just when you said how well I handled the situation –

Umbrella Woman With respect to him, yes. But now there is no cause for further concern.

Military Man Oh I think there is.

Umbrella Woman Oh I really think there isn't.

Military Man Why sure you don't. But if I'm honest, and I mean no offence, ma'am, I'm none too confident about how well you've handled things so far.

Umbrella Woman Pardon me?

Military Man Well, for one, you let Leaky Larry in the bathroom leave his spot at number one to go to the phone. For two you let this lady take a seat even though she's not waiting in the line –

Umbrella Woman Queue –

Military Man – take the last available seat that really ought to be for me. For three *you* let some girl leave her bag on a stool to mark her spot while she sits in the café. I mean is that really your idea of responsible leadership? To let her get a shot over me, who swore an oath to protect and serve? And finally for four, you have sat here for God knows how long next to a suspicious item in a public area?

Umbrella Woman Suspicious?

Military Man Why sure.

162   The Last Return

There could be anything in that bag. I mean, what was it you called her?

Umbrella Woman   I didn't call her anything.

Military Man   You did. You called her a violent something and a something something something.

Umbrella Woman (*remembering*)   An absolute weapon and a pig-eating psycho.

Military Man   Yes you did! And something else.

Umbrella Woman (*feeling pressure*)   A ... danger to the public.

But it wasn't me who said she could ... Believe me I did all I could.

Military Man   Did you even bother to say anything to the ticket person?

Umbrella Woman   Yes, who point blank refused to engage and can only intervene on 'matters of security'.

Military Man (*getting up*)   Well, if this does not constitute a matter of security, I don't know what does.

Umbrella Woman   Where are you going?

Military Man   I'm going to do what the good people of my homeland know how to do best: complain about the service.

Umbrella Woman   No! No! You are absolutely right. I have allowed myself to be made a total fool of since I got here. You must allow me to make amends. With your permission, I will handle this my way.

Military Man   Well, if you're sure you know what you're doing.

Umbrella Woman   Absolutely I do.

The **Umbrella Woman** *goes to her bag and takes out her tin.*

Umbrella Woman   Would you like a protein ball? They're homemade.

Military Man   Thanks.

The **Military Man** *takes one.*

She gets up and approaches the **Ticket Person** *and rings the bell. The* **Military Man** *sits.*

Umbrella Woman   Excuse me.

The **Military Man** *turns to the* **Woman in Pink** *and smiles.*

The **Woman in Pink** *regards him coolly.*

He smugly tosses the protein ball into his mouth. She watches him chew, then looks away.

Meanwhile, the **Ticket Person** *turns to the* **Umbrella Woman**.

Umbrella Woman   Hello.

Ticket Person   Good evening. The Oppenheimer is sold out tonight. If you wish to queue for a last-minute return, we will reissue the tickets ten minutes before the performance begins.

Umbrella Woman   No thanks. Actually, I would like to report a suspicious person who may be an absolute psycho, a dangerous pig and who is potentially harbouring a weapon. I feel it is my duty to report it as a matter of public safety as all of our lives could be in danger.

Ticket Person   A suspicious person, you say?

Umbrella Woman   I do.

The **Ticket Person** *takes down a blue folder marked 'Suspicious Persons'.*

Ticket Person (*noting*)   Go on.

Umbrella Woman   Certainly. The person was seen to be carrying a bag. Backpack type of configuration. Shoulder straps. Front pocket. Bold colours. Garish, if you like. No rest for the eye.

Quite aggressive design, such as one would associate with a dangerous underground movement or violent splinter group. If you see a person approach this bag, then that is the person of whom I speak.

Ticket Person (*writing*)   Shoulder straps. Colourful markings. Splinter group. We'll look into it.

Umbrella Woman   Thank you.

Ticket Person   You're welcome.

The **Ticket Person** *returns to work. The* **Umbrella Woman** *returns to her seat.*

Military Man   You did the right thing.

Umbrella Woman   Well, one must carry out one's civic duty in the interests of the common good.

164   The Last Return

(*Sitting, clocks his hands are empty.*) I have kept my place, that's all that matters. And now I have thwarted this woman's prospects of unfairly securing a ticket and restored order to the queue, I am looking forward to this evening immensely.

Military Man   Me too.

Umbrella Woman   I am sure you are. That is, if you are lucky enough to get a ticket. After me.

Military Man   Yes, that *would* be most fortunate for me.

—

If it were true. But seeing as I have been *given* this place by the guy with the newspaper *personally* before he left, that makes *me* number one.

Umbrella Woman   Ah, I see how you have misinterpreted his gesture of offering you his *stool*. If I remember correctly, it was merely his *stool* he offered you, not his *place*.

Military Man   Well, if I remember correctly, what the man said was, 'I have to pop out to the bathroom for a minute. Could I trouble you to keep my *place*?'

Umbrella Woman   Yes, but if *I* remember correctly from my customer service diploma, people very often mis-remember what they hear in order to galvanise a consensus around their own personal agenda. Subconsciously of course. So when the man with the newspaper asked you to keep his *stool*, what you thought you heard was his *place*, an abstract noun that suggests a much clearer advantage over its poorer cousin, the common noun, stool.

The **Newspaper Man** *returns.*

Military Man   Well, let's just see about that.

Newspaper Man (*to* **Military Man**)   Phew.

The **Newspaper Man** *waits for the* **Military Man** *to move but he does not.*

Newspaper Man   Em … you can hang on to the stool of you like … if you want just pop it down past the lady beside you, I will reassume my position.

Military Man   Huh?

Newspaper Man   The stool. You can have it. You can pop it down there to your place in the queue.

Military Man   But this is my place.

Newspaper Man   No it's not.

Military Man   Yes it is. You gave it to me.

Newspaper Man   No, no, no, what I said was –

Military Man   What you *said* was. 'I have to pop out to the bathroom for a *minute*. Could I trouble you to keep my *place*?' And I said I would.

Newspaper Man   But I was only gone a minute.

Military Man (*checking watch*)   You were gone for six and a half minutes, so you broke our deal.

Newspaper Man   Everyone knows what a minute means.

Military Man   Well, according to my military training, sir, a minute means exactly sixty seconds. Not one second more. Not one second less. People rely on me to know the difference.

(*Court martial mode.*) So when you asked me for my help, did you or did you not use the word 'minute'?

Newspaper Man   Eh, maybe –

Military Man   And the word 'keep'?

Newspaper Man   Yes but not in the way you mean.

Military Man   And the word 'place'?

Newspaper Man   Yes.

Military Man   When that time exceeded a minute, you broke that contract.

Newspaper Man   What contract? I never made any contract!

The **Military Man** *opens his jacket to reveal a recording device strapped to his chest. He presses play.*

Newspaper Man   *Actually … I have to pop to the bathroom for a minute. I feel a bit –*

Military Man   *Sure thing. When you gotta go, you gotta go.*

Newspaper Man   *Could I trouble you to keep my place?*

Military Man   *Not a problem.*

166   The Last Return

The **Military Man** *snaps off the tape player and puts it back in his pocket.*

Military Man   Case dismissed.

Newspaper Man (*to* **Umbrella Woman**)   You … why did you not intervene?

Umbrella Woman   I thought it best not to step in.

Newspaper Man   Ah!

Umbrella Woman   But I think you are handling it perfectly.

Newspaper Man (*to* **Military Man**)   You are not going to get away with this. Stay there.

Military Man   Oh, I will.

Newspaper Man   You … don't you move.

Military Man   Oh, I won't.

The **Newspaper Man** *marches up to the* **Ticket Person**. *He rings the bell.*

Newspaper Man   Excuse me.

Ticket Person   Good evening.

Newspaper Man   Hello –

Ticket Person   The Oppenheimer is sold out tonight.

Newspaper Man   Yes, I know. I –

Ticket Person   You can always wait in the queue and if there are any last-minute returns, we will reissue the tickets ten minutes before the perf –

Newspaper Man   I know all that. In fact I have *been* queuing for well over an hour. But then I went to the toilet you see, because I have a kidney condition, and that man took my pl –

Ticket Person   I am the ticket person, sir, I am not responsible for organising the queue. It is up to the queue to organise themselves.

Newspaper Man   I know. But this military man – he had a secret machine see –

Ticket Person   I am the ticket person.

The Last Return   167

Newspaper Man   And I said I'd only be a minute but he, he, he secretly recorded me saying 'minute' and used it against me –

Ticket Person   I repeat, I am the ticket person, sir. This type of complaint is not within the remit of my duties. My job is to sell tickets.

Newspaper Man   This is *about* tickets.

Ticket Person   No, it is not about tickets. It is about your place in the queue. I am the ticket person.

Newspaper Man   So you keep saying –

Ticket Person   Not the queueing police charged to investigate your petty squabble about how your trip to the toilet adversely affected your place in the queue.

Newspaper Man   Come on! It's me! I've been coming to this foyer for thirty-six nights in a row, and every night I have been number one in this queue. You *know* who I am.

Ticket Person   No I do not.

Newspaper Man   You don't remember *me?*

Ticket Person   Why should I?

Newspaper Man   That first night I came in I said hello, how are you and isn't it a lovely day. And then we had that wonderful chat about recyclable cat litter.

Ticket Person   Perhaps we did. Perhaps we didn't. That type of chitchat is standard in my trade: the gentle banter, a kindly remark about the climate, then some cutsie comment about a family pet or some ethical belief system. This is all, of course, designed to personalise our exchange, and elevate you in my esteem, to make our interaction more special, so that we have like some … *unique connection.* Like in another life we could have been friends: squash partners or pals from a knitting circle. Instead, all we have is a tenuous bond soldered through a common interest in feline sanitation systems. This is what you think sets you apart from everyone else looking for last-minute returns. So when it comes to the crunch, say for example if there was only *one* ticket available for the Oppenheimer tonight, and a throng of people at my desk, clawing over each other, all claiming to be first, I would cast an eye across the desperate rabble in search of *you*, my 'special friend', the man I so helplessly developed a personal bias for. Our knowing smiles would intertwine like

168   The Last Return

wild rose stems on a hedgerow, and I would grant you the one remaining ticket with a sloping wink.

—

Well, sadly the opposite is true. I am trained to be impervious to such charm offensives launched upon me daily by oily charmers such as you. And while I sympathise with regards to your bowel complaint –

Newspaper Man   Kidney condition.

Ticket Person   Kidney condition, whatever. If truth be told, if I were a cat, and you were my owner, I'd throw myself off the roof and pray for a nice sharp set of railings.

The **Newspaper Man** *appears to grow weak as if being slowly killed by the words.*

Ticket Person   And if you dropped down dead in front of me right now, I would still go home, turn on the TV and watch reruns of the Eurovision Song Contest while eating instant noodles and wearing my ex lover's unwashed pyjamas. And tomorrow, I wouldn't be able to pick your face out from a chorus line of cadavers. Even if you threatened me with a live crocodile. That's how little I'd remember you!

Newspaper Man (*breathless*)   Good God, what are you?

Ticket Person   I am the ticket person! It is my job to keep control of the ticketing system. It is not now nor ever will be my job to organise the queue. We expect civilised people intending to queue for a ticket to a civilised event in a civilised building to organise themselves in a civilised fashion. How many times must you be told! It's very simple really: the first person to arrive is number one, the next is number two and so on until everyone who has arrived looking for a ticket has a number respective to the order in which they came.

That is the system, professor toilet pussy man. Should you wish to reinterpret or corrupt the system, then you only have yourself to blame for its failure!

Newspaper Man   Right. Right. Right.

The **Newspaper Man** *goes to the seat with the backpack on it and lifts it off. He has urinated down one leg of his trousers.*

Umbrella Woman   Oh good heavens no!

The **Ticket Person** *watches through opera glasses.*

Military Man   What are you doing?

Newspaper Man   I am taking my place.

Umbrella Woman   That's not your place.

The **Ticket Person** *checks the blue folder.*

Newspaper Man   Who said it's not?

The **Ticket Person** *discreetly raises the receiver of the hotline.*

Umbrella Woman   You for one. You said it when you refused to let me sit on it when I came in.

Ticket Person (*into phone*)   Charlie, this is Alpha-Alpha Topsy-Turvy reporting a code blue situation.

Umbrella Woman   First you said you were *minding* it for a girl in the café. Then you *told* me I couldn't sit on it. Which is it to be?

Ticket Person   Subject is male.

Newspaper Man   I never said that.

Ticket Person   Carrying backpack.

Umbrella Woman   Oh, *now* you never said that?

Ticket Person   Agitated, sweating and incontinent.

Newspaper Man   I never said you couldn't sit on it. You were always free to take her place if you really wanted it. You heard the ticket person: it's up to the people in the queue to organise themselves. But you lacked the courage to do so. Whereas *I* do not.

Umbrella Woman   That place is mine.

The **Newspaper Man** *grabs the stool by one leg and uses it as a defence weapon / shield, still holding the backpack. The* **Woman in Pink** *looks up from her phone.*

Newspaper Man   Well, come and get it then, Nelly No Mates. 'Oh there's people at work and they're really mean to me … whaa, whaa, wha …'

Military Man   Now look –

We hear the low hum of a chopper approach. The **Woman in Pink** *removes her headphones and listens.*

170   The Last Return

Newspaper Man   And you can shut your strudel hole as well. You, having most recently joined the queue, have no mandate to upset the status quo.

We see a red laser dot appear on his body.

Newspaper Man   I was here first! Before any of you. Remember that. As newcomers, it is incumbent on you all to assimilate with the system that was set up by your queuing forebears, ergo my system!

The chopper sounds grow. Swirling red and blue lights fill the room from outside.

Megaphone   Sir.

Newspaper Man   A system which, I may add, has worked seamlessly prior to your arrival. If the culture of waiting we have set up here is not apt to suit your needs, I suggest you take yourself off somewhere else and find a queueing system more suited to your customs and lifestyle.

Megaphone   Step down off the chair, sir.

The **Newspaper Man** *lunges about the foyer, trying to dodge the laser beam.*

Newspaper Man   No! Get away! I am the king!

Megaphone (*to colleague*)   Target clear. Prepare to engage.

Newspaper Man   I am the king! And I will not be slain!

Megaphone   Put the bag down, sir.

Newspaper Man   Shuddup!

Megaphone   Put the bag down. That's an order.

Newspaper Man (*lifting bag*)   What? This?

Waving bag.

Megaphone   Do not agitate the bag, sir.

Newspaper Man   It's not even mine, you idiot! It belongs to a girl in the café –

We hear a high-velocity bullet or maybe a laser gun rip through the air. It hits the **Newspaper Man***, killing him. He slides down the upstage wall and slumps in a discreet heap away from the subsequent action. Everyone stares at the scene as the sound of the chopper fades away. We hear them talk over their chopper headsets, 'Good job, son – Nice shot – Let's go get a beer ...'*

The **Ticket Person** *returns to work. A pause as everyone else stares at the* **Newspaper Man**, *until all is silent, then turn to face front. The* **Woman in Pink** *no longer looks at her phone. She stares ahead too.*

The **Ticket Person***'s phone rings.*

Ticket Person   Hello, you are through to the box office for Oppenheimer's *Return to Hindenburg*. How may I help you? …Yes, the weather is dreadful this evening I know …

(*Making a note.*) And you were in …? Row M six and seven … And are you releasing the two seats or just the one?

Just … the … one.

The **Ticket Person** *hangs up. A thick silence descends. Eventually the* **Military Man** *casts his gaze down to the* **Newspaper Man**.

Military Man (*coolly*)   So the guy with the newspaper, he was first.

Umbrella Woman   He *was* first.

Umbrella Woman/Military Man   Now I am first.

They look at each other.

Umbrella Woman   I am first.

Military Man   I am first. I was the one who raised the alarm about the bag.

Umbrella Woman   But it was I who in the interests of public safety reported it to the ticket person as a danger to the public.

The **Military Man***'s charm ebbs.*

Military Man   But that was only because I convinced you into thinking it was so.

Umbrella Woman   *Au contraire, mon frère.* It was *I* who convinced *you* into thinking you were convincing *me* in order to make you think *you* had the upper hand when you didn't. But, then, maybe that's not true either.

Military Man   And now you're just trying to …

(*Coughs.*) … confuse the situation even more to get in ahead of me, aren't you?

Umbrella Woman   Maybe I am. Maybe I'm not. Maybe I am. Maybe I'm not.

Military Man (*sudden cough*)

Umbrella Woman   I'm sorry? You say something?

Military Man (*sudden choke*)

Umbrella Woman   What's that?

Military Man (*breathless*)

Umbrella Woman   I'm sorry I don't follow.

Military Man   Arr … agh … ugh … lar … rar … rar …

Umbrella Woman   Arraghughlararar? Are you alright? I can't quite make out what you said.

Military Man (*struggling to breathe, garbled talk*)   Ph … ool … ap … poop … shuuuu …

Umbrella Woman (*taking water*)   Something stuck? You need water. Here.

The **Military Man** *reaches to take the water but it falls.*

Umbrella Woman   Oh dear. Never mind.

He falls across her lap, and she holds him like a baby, rocking him as he struggles to breath. The **Woman in Pink** *watches.*

Umbrella Woman   There, there. That's it. Shush.You must be tired after coming such a long way.

As the **Woman in Pink** *watches, she slowly stands and takes a few steps away. She slides her hand into her pocket, pulls out the protein ball and regards it.*

Umbrella Woman   That's it. There you go. Nice and easy. There you go. Whoopsie daisies. That's it. Big sleepy now.

> When Letty had scarce pass'd her third glad year,
> And her young, artless words began to flow,
> One day we gave the child a colour'd sphere
> Of the wide earth, that she might mark and know,
> By tint and outline, all its sea and land.
> She patted all the world; old empires peep'd
> Between her baby fingers; her soft hand
> Was welcome at all frontiers. How she leap'd,

And laugh'd and prattled in her worldwide bliss;
But when we turn'd her sweet unlearnèd eye
On our own isle, she raise'd a joyous cry,
'Oh yes I see it, Letty's home is there!'
And, while she hid all England with a kiss,
Bright over Europe fell her golden hair.[*]

The **Military Man** *sees the protein ball in her hand and realises he's been poisoned.*
The **Woman in Pink** *lets the protein ball slide off her hand. She picks up the water.*

Military Man   P ... P ... P ...

Umbrella Woman   Protein balls? Didn't you like them? They're
homemade.

The **Military Man** *collapses on the ground and reaches out to the* **Woman in**
Pink *for the water. She doesn't move.*

Military Man   W ... W ... W ...

Umbrella Woman   What's the recipe? Oh let's see. Walnuts, peanuts,
hazelnuts, banana chips, sodium cyanide.

Desperate, the **Military Man** *looks up to the* **Woman in Pink** *who sees he*
wants the water but she doesn't move. Gasping, delirious, the **Military Man** *crawls,*
foaming at the mouth, weakening with each move. The **Umbrella Woman**
looks on.

Umbrella Woman   Where are you going? Ah, has your little girl come
out to play in the sand dunes of your mind? What is her name? Let's call
her Letty? Shall we?

The **Military Man** *lies dead at the* **Woman in Pink** *'s feet. The* **Umbrella**
Woman *stands and faces her.*

Umbrella Woman   Found who you were looking for?

The **Woman in Pink** *stares at the* **Umbrella Woman** *with the expression of*
someone who has seen off worse enemies.

Woman in Pink   I would like to tell you a story, if I may. Once a poor
man met a rich man at the gates of his farm to fight over a mountain
sheep.

'This sheep is mine,' said the poor man. 'Just because it strayed upon your
land, it does not mean it belongs to you.'

---

[*] 'Letty's Globe', by Charles Tennyson Turner.

174   The Last Return

'Yes,' said the rich man. 'But while the sheep was on my land, it ate my grass so it belongs to me.'

'You are wrong,' said the poor man. 'And now you will see.'

So he went into his house and returned with the rich man's son.

'Look who I found eating apples in my yard. If we are to follow your philosophy, your son belongs to me.'

'Please,' cried the rich man, 'give me back my son.'

'Please,' cried the poor man …

—

'Give me back my sheep.'

—

It is a common phenomenon among free-market economies to plunder the resources of the less fortunate and not feel remorse. As insignificant as these misdemeanours may seem, they build up. And up and up and up and up until the practice of forcing the poor to bend to the will of the rich becomes the norm. Then next thing you know … well, I refer you to the last four hundred years of European history, where the wealth of its nations was drawn with the blood of the innocent, and were by their very nature the mountain sheep of shame.

Umbrella Woman   You speak the language of commerce I see.

Woman in Pink   I speak five languages.

Umbrella Woman   I knew you were lying. From the second you walked in. I could tell by the way your eyes danced about your head like flies on a meat carcass.

Woman in Pink   But unlike you, I lied in pursuit of a nobler purpose.

Umbrella Woman   Which is?

Woman in Pink   To buy a ticket for the Oppenheimer at the concession rate for refugees, then resell on the street for six times the price.

Umbrella Woman   So you *have* come to trick us all and profit from your gain.

Woman in Pink   I have come to take back my sheep.

Umbrella Woman   Have you indeed?

The **Umbrella Woman** *picks up her umbrella.*

Umbrella Woman   Well, *I* took *two* buses to get here! *I* was here before you. *I* will be first in this queue and *you* are not going to stop me.

She pulls the handle of the umbrella away to reveal a sword.

The **Ticket Person** *looks through the opera glasses, then consults the catalogue of 'Suspicious Weapons' while the* **Woman in Pink** *is pursued by the* **Umbrella Woman**. *She grabs the mop out of the bucket in the corner, and uses it to defend herself.*

Woman in Pink   You took two buses to get here. I took sixty-three. The first I took with my daughter when a missile blew the roof off our home.

(*Swipe.*) Then we took a bus to Kenya, then Uganda, then Sudan, then to Libya where a fishing boat would take us on to Italy.

(*Swipe.*) But when we reached the shore, there were too many people trying to climb on board, and in the crush for a place, my daughter fell into the sea. She was pulled on board, and I was left behind, screaming out her name as they drifted out to sea. A man called out, 'Follow us to Amsterdam. Your daughter will be there.' So I waited for the next boat, and followed them to Amsterdam, but my daughter wasn't there.

(*Swipe.*) Then I took a bus to Spain and walked the streets of Madrid but my daughter wasn't there. Then I took a bus to France and walked the streets of Paris but my daughter wasn't there. Then I took a bus to Greece, and walked the streets of Athens but my daughter wasn't there. Then I walked the streets of London. Then I walked the streets of Brussels, I walked the streets of Berlin, I walked the streets of Vienna. Then I walked the streets of Rome.

(*Swipe.*) Street by street, year by year, seeking out her face. But I know I'll see her one day, because I taught her well: keep half of what they give you and profit from the rest.

The **Umbrella Woman** *pursues her like a rogue cyborg. They fight, retreat and circle each other again as the speech continues.*

Meanwhile, the **Ticket Person** *finds the item in the catalogue, lifts the receiver on the hotline and dials.*

Ticket Person (*to hotline*)   This is Alpha-Alpha T-T. Permission to engage.

Woman in Pink   So you can accuse me of abusing the system if you want, I don't care. Tonight I *will* succeed, because here's the truth, Umbrella Woman.

(*Swipe.*) I simply cannot fail.

The **Umbrella Woman** *trips the* **Woman in Pink** *and pounces on her. The* **Woman in Pink** *stops the descending weapon with her hands.*

Ticket Person   Copy that. Preparing response.

The **Ticket Person** *hangs up and disappears under the desk.*

The women continue to struggle on the floor.

Woman in Pink   I pretend I don't understand what you say, and beat the system just like you. Because if you had to go through what I went through to be here, you would know that queuing is for idiots. Instead you must scramble and push and shove and beg and grab and kick and punch and claw and trick and steal and shoot and stab your way to the front, because if you don't … You die!

The **Ticket Person** *reappears in swat gear and a sniper rifle or a laser gun, fires a shot and hits the* **Umbrella Woman**. *She slumps down dead.*

A pause.

Ticket Person (*sarcastic*)   If that's all you do.

The **Ticket Person** *puts away the assassination regalia efficiently.*

The **Woman in Pink** *pushes the* **Umbrella Woman** *off her and sits back on one of the stools, shocked, sad, exhausted.*

A pause.

We hear a cheery bing, bong, bing.

Ticket Person (*through a mic*)   The ticket office for tonight's performance of Oppenheimer's *Return to Hindenburg* is now open for last-minute returns. Anyone waiting for a last-minute return, please form an orderly queue at the ticket desk.

We hear a reprise of 'Ode to Joy', which begins gently but builds and swells as the following action unfolds.

Front of house staff enter and quietly clear the scene around the **Woman in Pink**.
*The bodies are stretchered off one by one and the stools are cleared until all that is left is
the* **Woman in Pink** *on the stool, and the backpack. A member of staff approaches.
She stands and her stool is removed. She puts the backpack on the floor and approaches
the* **Ticket Person**, *presents her ID, counts out three coins on the desk and purchases
the ticket. She heads for the exit when simultaneously ...*

A **Girl** *enters from the café carrying colouring books and crayons / study books. She goes
to the backpack, opens it, puts her things inside, puts it on her shoulder and approaches
the* **Ticket Person**. *The* **Woman in Pink** *turns back and sees her. The* **Girl**
*turns to face her. They both let their belongings fall to the floor, stretch out their arms
and run towards each other as the music swells to its crescendo. As they touch, the stage
curtains swish closed in time with the final bar of music.*

The End.